Independent Projects:
Step by Step

*A Handbook for Senior Projects,
Graduation Projects, and
Culminating Projects*

Patricia Hachten Wee

The Scarecrow Press, Inc.
Lanham, Maryland, and London
2000

SCARECROW PRESS, INC.

Published in the United States of America
by Scarecrow Press, Inc.
4720 Boston Way, Lanham, Maryland 20706
http://www.scarecrowpress.com

4 Pleydell Gardens, Folkestone
Kent CT20 2DN, England

British Library Cataloguing in Publication Information Available

Library of Congress Cataloging-in-Publication Data

Wee, Patricia Hachten, 1948–
    Independent projects, step by step : a handbook for senior projects,
    graduation projects, and culminating projects / Patricia Hachten Wee.
        p.   cm.
    Includes bibliographical references and index.
    ISBN 0-8108-3785-4 (alk. paper)
    1. Independent projects—United States—Handbooks, manuals, etc.
2. Project method in teaching—Handbooks, manuals, etc.   3. Twelfth
grade (Education)—United States.   I. Title.

    LB1620 .W42   2000
    373.139′43—dc21   00-024864

for my husband, Robert,
and our newest granddaughter,
Kiana Alyson Kolibas

Many thanks to the Media Center staff, Deb, Candy, Peggy, and Debbie. Special appreciation to Karen Leonhard for her unfailing assistance and support. Thanks to Polly Suzanne Leonhard for the joy of working with her over the years and for the best graduation project ever. And, as always, my love and gratitude to my husband, Robert—my idea source, my photographer, and *mi sol y mi sombra*.

CONTENTS

PART 1

USING INDEPENDENT PROJECTS

CHAPTER 1

What Is an Independent Project?

What is this thing called...

Whether it is called a Graduation Project, Senior Project, Senior Exit Project, or Culminating Project, an Independent Project is best described as a concentrated, in-depth study of a self-selected topic that falls outside the normal curriculum.

Across the United States and Canada, education reforms have led to a demand for demonstrations of competency as a requirement for high school graduation. In these schools all students, of all abilities, must give evidence of the capacity to find and use specific information, to independently develop and organize a complex project, to speak and write clearly, and to think critically. "Within the current focus on process-oriented, portfolio-evaluated, and authentic assessment methods, the [independent] senior project assignment hits the target."[1]

Educators and parents recognize that students possess a much wider range of abilities than is evident in conventional classroom settings. Independent Projects provide an educationally sound arena for exhibiting such abilities. The personal commitment to this kind of self-selected long-term assignment results in a genuine feeling of ownership of a substantial body of knowledge. Students gain confidence when they can demonstrate their expertise on a specific topic to a panel of adults.

This in-depth investigation of a topic "provides a context for taking the initiative and assuming responsibility, making decisions and choices, and pursuing interests."[2] Through independent projects students realize the necessity of the communication skills (grammar and vocabulary) they have been taught for so many years and that "research and learning are not dead-end tasks, but a means to an end."[3]

Additionally, recent research calls "for more cooperative efforts among student, staff member, parents, and community—and says we must train students for lifelong learning."[4] Independent Projects accomplish all that and more.

So, what type?

An Independent Project may be a requirement for graduation from high school, a requirement for a particular course, or some other requirement and may be evaluated by a classroom teacher or a panel of community members. Generally evaluated as a whole, an Independent Project normally includes a proposal, the project itself, an oral presentation, and a self-evaluation. Independent Projects are often graded on a pass/fail basis with an opportunity to re-do an unsatisfactory attempt.

Many schools encourage community involvement since there is often a need for experts outside the school and many incorporate a community-based panel of judges or evaluators. These factors are important since such societal involvement allows the students to view the Independent Project requirement more as a part of the real world and less as another school assignment. "In the real world, knowledge and skill are not fragmented, but integrated."[5]

Some schools require an Independent Project to encompass two or more content areas, some stipulate a service-related component, and some designate specific courses in which the project must be completed. Nevertheless, there is a general pattern to Independent Projects:

- choice of a self-selected topic,
- extension beyond the established curriculum,
- involvement of some type of research,
- analysis, synthesis, and application of information,
- documentation of time,
- production of a research-based paper with a works-cited page,
- creation of a product that is a natural extension of the topic,
- demonstration of the ability to communicate understanding,
- presentation to a class, a specialized group, or a panel of evaluators, and
- self-evaluation by the student.

Additionally, there may be requirements to:

- develop an organizational time line,
- incorporate audio visuals into the oral presentation,
- defend the work in a question-and-answer session, and
- find a particular kind of advisor and/or mentor.

My 1964 Karmann Ghia

Oregon, Arizona, Pennsylvania, and some provinces in Canada were among the first to make an Independent Project a requirement for graduation. Steven Baird[6] reports of a student who restored a 1964 Karmann Ghia for his graduation project. One can envision the student's research into original design engineering and restoration techniques and the panel of judges gathered around the restored car to hear the presentation.

Other Independent Projects students have completed include:

- writing, arranging, and recording an original jazz compositions,[7]
- breeding a strain of cotton to grow in the mid-Atlantic states and presenting the research at the International Science and Engineering Fair,
- studying the ballets of George Balanchine and choreographing an original ballet,
- producing a time management booklet for high school students,[8]
- learning sign language and videotaping the swimming instruction given to a deaf student,[9]
- discovering the cause of the many infant deaths over 150 years ago after observing the tombstones in a local cemetery.

An Independent Project may be one of the following or a combination:

1. **Analysis projects** involve in-depth research on an issue.

   This type of Independent Project requires substantial background research that will form the foundation for a unique interpretation or analysis of the topic. Students may conduct a survey and analyze the responses, design and complete an experiment, write an alter ego project, or analyze two sides to an issue in a pro and con format. Analysis projects require the preparation of a formal written report with documented references and the presentation of the analysis of the topic. Examples of analysis projects include science fair projects or research on a local issue of community concern.

2. **Exhibition projects** involve the demonstration of ability to produce some original piece of work.

   This type of Independent Project allows students to create and present their original composition for public appreciation. Students have the opportunity to apply skills in areas that are of intense personal interest, such as art, music, architecture, or graphic design. Example exhibition projects include a dance performance, an original poetry presentation, an art exhibit, or a show of fashion designs.

3. **Demonstration projects** involve learning new skills and displaying the results.

   This type of Independent Project encourages students to create, repair, or restore. Students will demonstrate the use of the appropriate tools or equipment, discuss or illustrate techniques, and present a finished product. Examples of demonstration projects include restoring a classic car, designing and building a greenhouse, or explaining and illustrating early photographic techniques.

Why bother?

Since the goal of every school is to send productive and literate citizens out into the world, we have to bother! Successful completion of Independent Projects provides "solid evidence that our kids can meet society's expectations,"[10] "instills the concept of lifelong learning, makes instruction relevant, integrates the curriculum, and attacks 'senioritis.'"[11] Furthermore, "a substantially higher level of writing is produced by freshmen who graduated from local high schools embracing the senior-project program than by others."[12]

After the release of the 1998 Third International Mathematics and Science Study (TIMSS), the expression "a mile wide and an inch deep" became a popular metaphor describing the science curriculum in the United States and its impact on student achievement.[13] The curriculum in many areas of instruction is frequently described by experts as rarely delving deeply into any single topic. Many state departments of education have mandated that students will apply, analyze, synthesize, and evaluate information and communicate significant knowledge and understanding.

Working through an Independent Project to its completion provides the student with life skills that will extend beyond school. *Science for All Americans*, the landmark collaboration of several hundred scientists, mathematicians, engineers, physicians, philosophers, historians, and educators, encourages emphasis on the exploration of questions, critical thinking, and acquisition of both knowledge of the world and scientific habits of mind in the education of young people.[3] Independent Project work, whether in science or in other fields, provides the student with ample opportunities to achieve the core knowledge and skills, stimulates critical thought processes, builds problem-solving skills, teaches the student to seek answers and to make quantitative observations, and fosters logical thinking, openness to new ideas, and informed skepticism.

Personal growth and satisfaction are additional goals associated with Independent Project work. Students derive a sense of accomplishment through the completion and 'ownership' of a body of work that is a reflection of personal interests and abilities. Independent Projects offer opportunities to expand individual knowledge, explore career paths, and apply learning to real-life situations that will serve to benefit the student's growth and promote lifelong learning.[14]

From an educators viewpoint, Independent Projects provide the perfect opportunity to institutionalize what education is all about—"students see learning in its totality, a journey from beginning to end with failures and successes along the road."[15]

Notes

1. Steven E. Baird, "Writing with Meaning in a Dispassionate Age," *English Journal* 81, no. 8 (Dec. 1992): 68.

2. Lilian G. Katz, "The Project Approach," Washington, DC: ERIC Clearinghouse on Elementary and Early Childhood Education (1994): 1.

3. Jane Summers, "The Senior Project: A Walkabout to Excellence," *English Journal* 78, no. 4 (April 1989): 63.

4. Deana R. Chadwell, "Show What You Know," *The American School Board Journal* (April 1991): 35.

5. Summers, "The Senior Project," 63.

6. Baird, "Writing with Meaning," 67.

7. Baird, "Writing with Meaning," 66.

8. Chadwell, "Show," 35.

9. Patsy Troutman and Connie Pawlowski, "The Senior Project: A Chance for the Library to Shine," *The Book Report* (Jan./Feb. 1997): 21.

10. Chadwell, "Show," 35.

11. Troutman and Pawlowski, "The Senior Project," 21.

12. Baird, "Writing with Meaning," 66.

13. Dan Freedman, "Science Education: How Curriculum and Instruction Are Evolving," *Curriculum Update* (Fall 1998): 1.

14. Summers, "The Senior Project," 62.
15. Summers, "The Senior Project," 65.

CHAPTER 2

Ideas for Teachers

Since teachers are frequently the advisors for Independent Projects and librarians (Library Media Specialists) are commonly the research experts, they shoulder the greatest responsibilities for ensuring the successful completion of these projects. One of the main purposes for this book is to provide these professionals with an easy way to do this part of their job.

This chapter is devoted to the specific needs of the teacher and the next chapter (chapter 3) provides assistance to the librarian. Chapter 4 outlines the steps in using this book and furnishes checklists to monitor student progress.

What is my role?

As an Independent Project advisor, the classroom teacher will consult regularly with the student to choose a topic, plan techniques, solve problems, and critique progress.

The advisor is the facilitator and first-line resource person whose tasks often include:

- ensuring that the project is within the student's capabilities,
- suggesting possible resources,
- determining that projects are appropriate, manageable, and realistic in time and scope,
- explaining the specific components of the project such as the written proposal, the oral presentation. and the self-evaluation,

- supervising deadlines,
- reviewing the various components,
- suggesting improvements,
- assisting with the formation of the evaluation criteria,
- cheerleading on tough days,
- aiding the student in arranging the presentation,
- evaluating the project in its entirety, which may include the proposal, the self-evaluation, the final or end product, and the oral presentation, and
- a lot of problem solving!

Inherent in these responsibilities is the need to ensure that the project is safe for the student and adheres to ethical and safety regulations. With questionnaires, surveys, and behavioral projects, the advisor must be certain that the proposed work conforms to federal regulations to safeguard the right and welfare of individuals who participate as research subjects. Appendix A contains project approval forms, informed consent forms, progress checklists, and evaluation forms to make the advisor's tasks easier to manage.

The logical steps of an Independent Project are generally defined as:

1. describe a problem or project,
2. pose questions,
3. locate and use information or human resources,
4. test strategies and apply information,
5. produce an end product,
6. present the product and conclusions, and
7. evaluate the process and product.

The purpose of completing an Independent Project is to show that the student can apply, analyze, synthesize, and evaluate information or utilize skills to produce an end product and communicate significant knowledge and understanding to others. The Independent Project must encompass academically challenging expectations for the individual student. As a general rule an Independent Project involves a minimum of twenty hours of work outside the curriculum with documentation of the time spent. In many school districts only students with individual education plans (IEPs) are exempt.

Getting started

The selection of a topic is always the hardest part for a student. Since an Independent Project requires so much time, effort, and commitment, the topic must be one that will maintain the student's interest. The topic needs to be rich enough to maintain the student's interest and broad enough to enable the student to devote twenty or more hours to its development. It "must be complex and comprehensive enough to challenge" and "have enough depth of cumulative knowledge that the student can analyze, apply, and synthesize."[1] Part 4 provides many sample projects and a list of other ideas in various content areas to assist in the selection of a topic.

Ideas for topics can be found in the sources listed in the bibliography, on the Internet, in newspapers and magazines, and on television. The explanations of the various steps involved in an Independent Project and the worksheets in chapter 4 will assist the student in finding a topic of interest. The advisor's task is to steer the student into choosing the best among his or her choices. With greater experience and knowledge, the advisor can usually foresee which topic has the greatest potential.

Finding resources

The first resource is the school librarian. Chapter 3 is devoted to assisting the school library media specialist in preparing to meet the specific needs of students as they develop and complete Independent Projects.

Other resources include universities and service organizations that often have directories of faculty and members with specific areas of expertise. These may also offer a source of community-based panels of evaluators or judges and of mentors for students requiring outside experts.

Exercise diligence when directing students to the Internet. Most schools have specific Internet usage regulations and guidelines that should keep students from encountering web sites that are unsuitable. Additionally, the advisor must make the student aware that some information found on the Internet is of a questionable nature. Require the student to support any report or data they glean from the Internet with more conventional sources.

Similar precautions should be taken when the student utilizes e-mail. The advisor may wish to make the initial contact so that professionals will not be inundated with unproductive messages such as "I am interested in France. Do you know how I can do a project on it?"

For the student who selects an Independent Project beyond the scope of the school's curriculum, a mentor outside the school may be needed. The mentor will assume some of the advisor's responsibilities and can be a community member or a relative of the student. The mentor acts as the subject area specialist and counselor who may suggest courses of action, resources, or other areas of focus. Some schools require the student to seek a mentor for the Independent Project, while others may suggest that the advisor contact possible experts.

Planning the phases

As Sylvia Chard notes, "In a sense, like a good story, the [Independent] project can be described as having a beginning, a middle, and an end, each memorable in its own way."[2] All multistage work entails development in three parts: the design and planning, the implementation and development, and the final draft and presentation/publication. Use of the step-by-step method presented in this book and the worksheets for each phase will provide a logical flow for the planning, development, and presentation of an Independent Project.

What to do with it

Once the student has selected a topic, you will surely be asked: "OK, now what do I do with it?" How do you help the student apply, analyze, and synthesize the information gleaned from research on the topic to produce an end product that is the basis of the presentation that will be evaluated by that panel of adults? While the product is a natural outgrowth of the topic choice of an exhibition-type project, a certain amount of ingenuity is required to find a tangible product for other kinds of projects. Giving some examples is the best way to get the idea across to students:

- an advertising campaign for a new snack item that the student developed,
- a sculpture created in the style of a famous sculptor,
- a sample plant of experimentally bred pest-resistant corn,
- a prom gown, designed and sewn by the student,
- a mannequin outfitted in a restored World War I uniform.

How do you help students incorporate their research on the topic into a product? Each sample project in part 4 provides several ideas for the product and the presentation. Focusing on the student's hobbies, skills, and interests may help. For example, a student who does not have a real gift for the art of photography, but loves to take pictures could use a photographic display for the product of nearly any topic. Other possible end products that can be used with a variety of topics are:

- storyboards,
- diaries,
- computer presentations,
- brochures created with desktop publishing software,
- videorecordings,
- slide presentations,
- role playing.

Giving the presentation

While the judges or evaluators will review the student's paper, the most critical part of an Independent Project is the presentation. As in other parts of an Independent Project, your school may have specific requirements.

The end product plays a central role in the presentation. Students who are proud of the product they have created find it much easier to design a quality presentation and to make the presentation with confidence. Practicing frequently in front of family, friends, or the advisor is helpful. If possible, videorecord practice sessions for the student to critique.

Ideas for the presentation often grow naturally from the product. A PowerPoint (Microsoft) slideshow of a student's research on ancient uses of kenaf fiber *is* the presentation. A program of photographic slides or overhead transparencies can be used with most topics. While students are overly fond of producing videorecordings, you will need to set specific guidelines for them. It is wise to periodically review the video and to keep the final copy in your hands until it is inserted in the machine to show the panel of judges.

Presentations are generally 10 to 15 minutes in length. Most schools suggest including a few minutes for questions from the judges; some require a serious defense of the student's work. Assistance from the public speaking teacher may be useful.

The research paper

A research-based paper that applies the knowledge gained in the research is required for any type of Independent Project. The format of the paper and the bibliography will depend upon the field of research: a comparative study of works of literature should be written according to your language arts department guide; the paper accompanying a science fair project should follow the format of scientific journals; whereas, a report on a technology education project should follow the generalized guidelines of report writing.

Most schools require the research paper for an Independent Project to be a minimum of five pages. While students usually have substantial experience in writing papers or reports, they may need assistance in following the specific format or in lengthening or shortening the paper. You can increase the motivation for writing a quality paper by reminding the student that this work may provide a competitive edge for college acceptance or a job.

Student and advisor evaluations

Students are usually required to make their own evaluation of their Independent Project. This self-evaluation may take the form of a brief essay that tells

- what the student learned in the completion of the project,
- how the project met the student's self-selected evaluation criteria,
- if the project were to be continued or refined, what would have to be done, and
- what impact or value the project had.

The advisor's evaluation may be written easily from the completed checklists of the student's progress.

Portfolios?

Independent Projects are an ideal way to complete a portfolio requirement. An Independent Project "provides a format for students to compile their best work and their finest accomplishments."[3] By the time students complete their projects there will be a wealth of material to include in the portfolio:

- the documentation of the selection, refinement, and development of the topic,
- the project proposal,
- the evolution of the topic research,
- the time line,
- the research paper,

- the end product and excerpts of the presentation or photographs taken of the product during or before the presentation,
- judges comments,
- the student's and advisor's evaluation.

Notes

1. Patsy Troutman and Connie Pawlowski, "The Senior Project: A Chance for the Library to Shine," *The Book Report* (Jan./Feb. 1997): 20.

2. Sylvia C. Chard, *The Project Approach* (Edmonton, Alberta, Canada: The University of Alberta, 1992): 10.

3. Donna Dermond, "Reference Guide for Senior Seminar: A Curriculum Development Project" (n.p. 1991): 65.

CHAPTER 3

Ideas for Librarians

School library media specialists (librarians) find Independent Projects a convenient avenue by which to integrate the library program with all curriculum areas, as well as with nearly every step of the projects—from topic selection and refinement to preparation of the presentation.

Librarians ARE resources

Students and teachers rely on librarians to supply references on all sorts of topics. Building the students' interest and helping them find topics are the first steps in getting students started with their Independent Projects. The librarian will be besieged with requests for books and periodicals for several weeks. Arranging flexible access to the Media Center and setting out many of the resources at your disposal (project idea books, current magazines, historical periodicals, general references, etc.) will help the advisors and the students with this all-important first step.

Use of Internet sites can be helpful in the research for Independent Projects, but be certain to caution students that some material may be of questionable authenticity and value.

Librarians guide the research

"In teaching students and teachers about selecting and using information, school library media specialists will act as resource guides or facilitators, imparting valuable, transferable information management skills."[1]

When Debra Kachel discusses the role of the school librarian in teaching students and teachers, she lists some examples of skills and tasks which school library media specialists will need to add to their repertoire in the "wall-less library."

- to know what resources are attainable from other libraries and information services and how long it takes to obtain them
- to know which formats are best for which learning styles or informational needs
- to diagnose and match needs with resources whether it is a book in the collection or a document in a database accessible through the Internet
- to recommend or create bookmarks of sites on the Internet with reliable, useful information which match the curriculum
- to assist students and teachers with technical difficulties in using electronic resources (i.e., downloading to disk, using "plug-in" software to play video clips from the Internet, creating hyper media documents)
- to seek out and form resource-sharing agreements with other libraries and engage in cooperative collection development activities
- to understand the cost-efficiency of document delivery knowing when to use ILL, online full-text database vendors, and commercial document delivery services.[2]

When the students move on to researching their topics and writing their papers, you may want to again set out collections of books in the Media Center. Encourage the advisors to provide you with a list of their students' topics in order to allow you to search for the most helpful resources.

The Internet can offer more than just background information on projects. It can provide fascinating glimpses into the world of professionals and possibilities of communicating with "real" scientists, historians, economists, architects, artists, writers, entrepreneurs, engineers, chefs, politicians, and many others. Students can also make virtual visits to universities, museums, and a wide range of organizations.

Providing resources for Independent Projects on a great diversity of topics "greatly impacts collection development."[3] The use of interlibrary loans can help offset deficits in budget-limited collections.

Advisors will look to librarians for guidance with proper paper format, bibliographic style, and research sources for difficult topics. All of these instances promote a more meaningful working relationship among students, teachers, librarians, and members of the local community.

Librarians provide creativity

The creative abilities of librarians can make a critical difference in students' projects and presentations. In many schools the Media Center becomes the workcenter for planning and designing the presentations and the products. Librarians are often the resident experts for assisting students with computer software to craft their visual displays, with scanning photographs into the computer, and with transferring relevant materials from the Internet.

Depending upon the layout of your school, the library may even serve as the site for the judging of the projects. This arrangement can offer you another opportunity to showcase the vast resources available in the Media Center. This is good public relations since "community participants can see their tax dollars at work in the library."[4]

Notes

1. Debra E. Kachel, *Collection Assessment and Management for School Librarians* (Westport, CT: Greenwood Press, 1997), 95.

2. Kachel, *Collection Assessment*, 95.

3. Patsy Troutman and Connie Pawlowski, "The Senior Project: A Chance for the Library to Shine," *The Book Report* (Jan./Feb. 1997): 20.

4. Troutman and Pawlowski, "The Senior Project," 21.

CHAPTER 4

How To Use This Book

This book was written to provide students, teachers, librarians, and administrators with an easy-to-use method of incorporating Independent Projects into the high school curriculum. The steps and worksheets in part 2, "The Independent Project Handbook," are guides to completing worthwhile projects with minimum frustration and procrastination. Part 3 follows two Independent Projects from topic selection to presentation. Part 4 provides one-page synopses of sample Independent Projects and lists of ideas for other projects by content area.

Following the steps and worksheets in part 2 will enable the student to produce an independent project that

- focuses on and evolves from a concise topic,
- reflects good organizational skills,
- draws upon appropriate supporting information,
- communicates significant knowledge, and
- culminates in an interesting end product and presentation.

It is recommended that the Independent Project advisor and the student set specific deadlines for the completion of each step and read through the completed projects in part 2 before beginning an individual project. As the student develops each worksheet for his or her own project, reference to the steps in each example project can again be of assistance.

Appendix A contains a sample Independent Project Approval form to be completed after the project proposal is written. It is suggested that a specific administrator be designated to sign and that the school nurse be enlisted to approve the safety of the project. An Informed Consent form is included for use with projects that involve human subjects. The checklists in appendix A provide the advisor with a convenient method to track the student's progress and allow for conferences at logical points during the progress of the project. A sample evaluation form is also included. Appendix B offers a list of books of ideas for projects.

Many of the presentation ideas and end products listed in the sample projects in part 3 can be used with Independent Projects in entirely unrelated content areas. A brainstorming session between the advisor and the student will often produce sufficient possibilities for both the presentation and the product.

References

American Association for the Advancement of Science. *Benchmarks for Science Literacy, Project 2061.* New York: Oxford University Press, 1993.

Ancess, Jacqueline, and Linda Darling-Hammond. *The Senior Project: Authentic Assessment at Hodgson Vocational/Technical High School.* A Series on Authentic Assessment and Accountability. Columbia University, New York. Teachers Collection National Center for Restructuring Education, Schools and Teaching. 1994.

Baer, John. *Creativity and Divergent Thinking.* Hillside, NJ: Erlbaum, 1993.

Baird, Steven E. "Writing with Meaning in a Dispassionate Age." *English Journal* 81, no. 8 (Dec. 1992): 66-68.

Bell, John T. "Implementation of Multiple Interrelated Projects within a Senior Design Course." *Chemical Engineering Education* 30, no. 3 (Summer 1996): 204-209.

Benafel, Linda. "Portfolio Assessment of Literature-Based Multimedia Presentations." *The Writing Notebook* 10, no. 3 (Jan./Feb 1993): 4-6.

Chadwell, Deana R. "Show What You Know." *The American School Board Journal* (April 1991): 34-35.

————. "The Senior Project: South Medford High School, Medford, Oregon." *Exemplary Practices in Education* (April 1992): 8-9.

Chard, Sylvia C. *The Project Approach.* Edmonton, Alberta, Canada: The University of Alberta, 1992.

Cowen, Sue, and Duncan Carter. "The Senior Project and the English Curriculum of the Future." *English Journal* 83, no. 4 (April 1994): 57-60.

Cuthbert, Katherine. "Project Planning and the Promotion of Self-Regulated Learning: From Theory to Practice." *Studies in Higher Education* 20, no. 3 (Oct. 1995): 267-277.

Dermond, Donna. *Reference Guide for Senior Seminar. A Curriculum Development Project.* n.p. Jan. 1991.

Dickinson, James. "The Senior Project at Rider College." *Teaching Sociology* 21, no. 3 (July 1993): 215-218.

Elizabethtown Area School District. *Graduation Project Handbook.* Elizabethtown, PA, 1995.

Elmore, R. "On Changing the Structure of Public Schools." In *Restructuring Schools,* ed. R. Elmore. San Francisco: Jossey-Bass, 1990.

Ephrata Area School District. *Graduation Project.* Ephrata, PA, n.d.

Etobicoke School District. *Making the Grade: Evaluating Student Progress.* Etobicoke, Canada, n.d.

Freedman, Dan. "Science Education: How Curriculum and Instruction Are Evolving." *Curriculum Update* (Fall 1998): 1-8.

Glendale Union High School District. *Exit Outcomes Assessment: Senior Study.* Glendale, AZ, 1993.

Gurau, Yolanda, and Joe Bartelme. "Testing the Technology Student's Skills with Applied Design Projects." *Engineering Education* 81, no. 5 (July-Aug. 1991): 487-490.

Herrnstein, R., and C. Murray. *The Bell Curve.* New York: Free Press, 1994.

Huse, Edgar, and Thomas Hummings. *Organizational Development and Change.* San Francisco: West Publishing Company, 1995.

Joyce, Bruce, and Marsha Weil. *Models of Teaching.* 5th Edition. Boston: Allyn and Bacon, 1997.

Kachel, Debra E. *Collection Assessment and Management for School Librarians.* Westport, CT: Greenwood Press, 1997.

Kandel, Eric R., and Robert D. Hawkins. "The Biological Basis of Learning and Individuality." *Scientific American* 267 (Sept. 1992): 79-86.

Katz, Lilian G. "The Project Approach." Washington, DC: ERIC Clearinghouse on Elementary and Early Childhood Education, 1994.

LoGiudice, Jim. *Meeting the Graduation Project Requirement: Considerations for Implementation.* Bucks County Intermediate Unit. Workshop Presentation. December 3, 1993.

Louis, K. S., and M. B. Miles. *Improving the Urban High School.* New York: Teachers College Press, 1990.

Magner, Denise K. "At St. Mary's College, Seniors Embark on Journeys within Their Majors." *Chronicle of Higher Education* 38, no. 39 (June 3, 1992): A13-14.

Maryland Department of Education. *Group Graduation Project.* Maryland School Performance Assessment Program, nd.

Mitchell, Ruth, Marilyn Willis, and the Chicago Teachers Union Quest Center. *Learning in Overdrive.* Golden, CO: North American Press, 1995.

Pennsylvania Department of Education. *Code Chapter 4*, 1998.

Rutherford, F. James. *Science for All Americans, Project 2061.* New York: Oxford University Press, 1994.

Sarason, Seymore Bernard. *The Predictable Failure of Educational Reform: Can We Change Course before It's Too Late?* San Francisco: Jossey-Bass, 1990.

Simmons, Gail C. "Experiential Education in the English Classroom." In *Experience and the Curriculum*, ed. Bert Horwood. Boulder, CO: Association for Experiential Education; Dubuque, IA: Kendal Hunt Pub. Co., 1995.

Sommers, Jonita. "Statistics in the Classroom: Written Projects Portraying Real-World Situations." *Mathematics Teacher* 85, no. 4 (April 1992): 310-313.

Smith, Marilyn. "A Community-History Project." *Journal of the Assembly of Rural Teachers of English* (1993): 14-16.

Summers, Jane. "The Senior Project: A Walkabout to Excellence." *English Journal* 78, no. 4 (April 1989): 62-64.

Troutman, Patsy, and Connie Pawlowski. "The Senior Project: A Chance for the Library to Shine." *The Book Report* (Jan./Feb. 1997): 20-21.

Warren, Ellen. "Senior Project's Tailor-made for Prom." *Chicago Tribune*, June 2, 1995. page 2, Metro DuPage section, DuPage Sports Final edition.

Wiggins, Grant. "Teaching to the Authentic Test: The Exhibition of Mastery." *Educational Leadership* 46, no. 7 (April 1989): 41-47.

Williamson, Susan, et al. "Roots in the Classroom." *The Book Report* 9, no. 3 (Nov.-Dec. 1990): 31-34.

Wee, Patricia Hachten. *Managing Successful Science Fair Projects: Step by Step.* Portland, ME: J. Weston Walch, 1996.

———. *Science Fair Projects for Elementary Schools: Step by Step.* Lanham, MD: Scarecrow Press, 1998.

Wee, Patricia Hachten, and Mary Ann Hagen. "Elementary Science Fairs: Collaboration between Teachers and School Library Media Specialists." *School Library Media Activities Monthly* XV, no. 7 (March 1999): 27-29.

PART 2

THE INDEPENDENT PROJECT HANDBOOK

The Independent Project Handbook

- ◆ **Step 1**   **Selecting a Topic**
    - **Worksheet 1: Selecting a Topic**
- ◆ **Step 2**   **Refining Your Topic**
    - **Worksheet 2: Refining Your Topic**
- ◆ **Step 3**   **Developing Your Topic into a Project**
    - **Worksheet 3: Developing Your Topic into a Project**
- ◆ **Step 4**   **Choosing an Advisor**
    - **Worksheet 4: Choosing an Advisor**
- ◆ **Step 5**   **Selecting a Mentor**
    - **Worksheet 5: Selecting a Mentor**
- ◆ **Step 6**   **Constructing a Time Line**
    - **Worksheet 6: Constructing a Time Line**
- ◆ **Step 7**   **Researching Your Topic**
    - **Worksheet 7: Researching Your Topic**
- ◆ **Step 8**   **Writing Your Proposal**
    - **Worksheet 8: Writing Your Proposal**
- ◆ **Step 9**   **Writing Your Paper**
    - **Worksheet 9: Writing Your Paper**
- ◆ **Step 10**   **Designing Your Presentation**
    - **Worksheet 10: Designing Your Presentation**
- ◆ **Step 11**   **Making Your Self-Evaluation**
    - **Worksheet 11: Making Your Self-Evaluation**

Step 1: Selecting a Topic

This Independent Project offers you the opportunity to finally choose your own topic. What are some of the things you've always wished your teachers would let you study? Come on, I know you've said (at least in your mind) "why can't we learn about _____?" Maybe you would fill in the blank with cars, fashion, parachuting, computers, marine biology, photography, or Civil War history.

You can develop any of these topics into an original project with all the necessary parts required by your school. Generally Independent Projects are composed of:

- a student-selected topic,
- a written proposal,
- activities necessary to complete the project (fieldwork, experiments, literary research, survey, etc.),
- documentation of the work done and sources used,
- an end product,
- an oral presentation of the product and conclusions,
- a self-evaluation, and
- an advisor evaluation.

The worksheets that follow will help you develop your chosen topic into an independent project.

Worksheet 1: Selecting a Topic

To help you pick a topic for your project, complete the following:

- List 3 things you've always wondered about:
    1._____
      _____
    2._____
      _____
    3._____
      _____

- List 3 things you've always wanted to know more about:
    1._____
      _____
    2._____
      _____
    3._____
      _____

- I love to read about:
    _____
    _____

- If you could be someone else for just one day, who would you be?
    _____
    _____

- If you could live in another time, when would it be?
    _____
    _____

Which of these ideas can you picture yourself working on for 4 months or more? You'll have to read a lot about it, do some original research or develop a particular focus, explain it to experts and laypeople; and if you really want to make it a worthwhile experience—*breathe it!*

Choose one of these for your project topic.

_____
_____
_____

Step 2: Refining Your Topic

Now you have to turn your topic into an entire project. The project will need to be ambitious enough to encompass the amount of time (typically about 20 hours) and the specific components (usually a paper and an oral presentation) that your school or class requires.

You may have to make some adjustments to your choice of topic.

♦ CHOOSE ANOTHER TOPIC:

• IF one encyclopedia article covers the topic.
You will not be able to develop this topic into a project if you can find out everything there is to know about the subject in one article. A student was very fond of giraffes, but when he started researching, he found that one entry in an encyclopedia covered just about all there was to know.

• IF the topic will not keep your interest for several months.
You will not be able to make this topic into a project if there's only one aspect about the topic that interests you. A student really enjoyed reading romance novels, but she didn't like to write stories or read the real history of exotic lands or different times.

♦ REFINE YOUR TOPIC

• IF the topic is too broad.
You will not have a good project if there are hundreds of books in the library on the subject. A student chose birds for her topic and found that this is much too broad a topic. She had to narrow her interest to the nesting behavior of predatory birds in order to produce a quality project.

• IF you cannot write a specific question that your project will answer.
You will not have a good project if you have trouble constructing a one-sentence question for the focus of your project. A student narrowed his topic to the decline of amphibian populations is the world. When he began to write the focus of his project he could not refine this idea into one concise sentence. This is symptomatic of having chosen too broad or too vague a topic.

Refine your topic on Worksheet 2 on the next page.

Worksheet 2: Refining Your Topic

Write the topic you have tentatively chosen:

_____

_____

Complete the following about your topic:

Does one encyclopedia article tell just about everything there is to know about your topic?

_____

(If the answer is "yes," you should choose another topic.)

• Can you spend an hour a day for several months enjoying your topic?

_____

(If the answer is "no," you should pick another topic.)

• Approximately how many books are in the library on your topic?

_____

(If the number of books is over 30, you should narrow the scope of your topic.)

• Approximately how many magazine articles are in the library on your topic?

_____

(If the number of articles is over 50, you should narrow the scope of your topic.)

• Write one sentence to explain the focus of your project.

_____

_____

_____

_____

_____

_____

(If you have difficulty putting the idea for your project into one sentence, consider another way to approach the topic or another aspect of the topic on which to focus. You may need to ask your advisor for assistance.)

Step 3: Developing Your Topic into a Project

Now that you have refined your topic, you need to develop the idea into a project. Carefully read the specific requirements for the project set by your school or class. Generally, a project consists of:

- a proposal,
- a logbook of time spent and sources used,
- a written report,
- end product,
- an oral presentation to a group,
- a self-evaluation, and
- an advisor evaluation.

Before you can move ahead with your project, you need to think about the direction you want your project to take and how you envision your project unfolding. In other words, think about the big picture. Much of what you develop in this step will be useful in writing your Independent Project proposal and in finding a suitable advisor. For you proposal you will need to explain:

- the reason you choose your topic from your Worksheet 1,
- what you want to learn about your topic,
- how you will go about learning this,
- what sources you can use,
- how you will document the time you spend developing your project,
- what your end product will be, and
- what kind of presentation you will make.

The following definitions may help you decide what type of project yours will be. An Independent Project may be one of the following or a combination:

1. **Analysis projects** involve in-depth research on an issue.

    This type of Independent Project requires substantial background research that will form the foundation for a unique interpretation or analysis of the topic. You may conduct a survey and analyze the responses, design and complete an experiment, write an alter ego project, or analyze two sides to an issue in a pro and con format. Analysis projects require the preparation of a formal written report with documented references and the presentation of the analysis of the topic. A science fair project is an example of an analysis project. The end product in this case would be the three-dimensional science fair project presented at the science fair and judged there. Another example of an analysis project is research on a local issue of community concern. In this case the end product could be highlights of the research results presented on overhead transparencies.

2. **Exhibition projects** involve the demonstration of ability to produce some original piece of work.

    This type of Independent Project allows you to create and present an original composition for public appreciation. You have the opportunity to apply skills in areas that are of intense personal interest, such as art, music, architecture, or graphic design. Examples of exhibition projects include a dance performance, an original poetry presentation, an art exhibit, or a show of fashion designs. The end product of exhibition projects is the original piece of work you produced.

3. **Demonstration projects** involve learning new skills and displaying the results.

    This type of Independent Project encourages you to create, repair, or restore. You will demonstrate the use of the appropriate tools or equipment, discuss or illustrate techniques, and present a finished product. Examples of demonstration projects include restoring a classic car, designing and building a greenhouse, or explaining early photographic techniques. The end product of a demonstration project is the item you created, repaired, or restored.

At this point you need to describe what you will do with your topic that will be different or unusual—what it is that will make your project unique. For example, can you accomplish one of the following and develop it into your end product?
- do an actual experiment,
- conduct a survey,
- create a piece of artwork,
- make a novel comparison,
- build a better engine,
- improve an existing product,
- do some unusual fieldwork, or
- develop an alter ego (a persona to help your idea unfold).

You also need to think about ideas that you have for your presentation. Would you like to develop a presentation based upon:
- a computer slideshow?
- a photograph album?
- a videorecording?
- a cartoon or storyboard?
- a booklet or brochure?
- a scrapbook or diary?

Worksheet 3: Developing Your Topic into a Project

Write your topic.

_____

_____

_____

- Write the purpose; the sentence that explains your project (from Worksheet 2).

_____

_____

_____

- Give a reason for selection of your topic.

_____

_____

_____

- What do you want to learn about your topic?

_____

_____

_____

_____

_____

_____

- How will you go about learning this?

_____

_____

_____

_____

- What sources can you use?

_____

_____

_____

_____

- Describe what you will do with the topic that will make your project unique (an experiment, an unusual comparison or fieldwork) and your end product.

_____

_____

_____
_____
_____
_____

• How will you document the work you do? (experimental data book, diary, journal)

_____
_____
_____
_____
_____

• What ideas do you have for your presentation?

_____
_____
_____
_____
_____

Step 4: Choosing an Advisor

The next step in your project will be choosing an advisor for you unless one has been assigned to you. Determine what requirements your school has for the Independent Project advisor. Some schools require that your project be presented in a specific class: this, of course, will limit your choice of advisors. In other schools, students are able to fulfill their project requirement in many different ways.

- IF you must complete your project in a specific class, you should complete Section 1 of Worksheet 4 now.
- IF you have a choice of how you will present your project, continue reading this section before proceeding to Worksheet 4.

Generally, a project advisor is a teacher or community member who meets with the student on a regular basis to plan techniques, solve problems, and critique the progress of your project. This adult may or may not be an expert on the topic you have chosen. If you require expert help for your project, you may need to find a mentor in addition to your advisor (see Step 5: Mentor). Your advisor will:

- suggest possible resources,
- consult with you regularly on your plan and progress,
- review and explain each step of your project,
- discuss deadlines,
- approve your proposal form,
- sign appropriate forms,
- assist in arranging for your presentation, and
- evaluate your project.

Worksheet 4: Choosing an Advisor

SECTION 1: Complete this section only if a project advisor has been assigned to you.
My Project Advisor is _____
My advisor's office hours (or times when we can meet):

_____

_____

SECTION 2: Complete this section only if you must choose a project advisor.

1. Do I need an advisor who is familiar with my topic? _____
2. Are there teachers in my school who meet this criterion? (You may have to talk
    to other students or to teachers or administrators to determine this). _____
    (If the answer is "no," you should choose a mentor in addition to a project
    advisor. Proceed to Step 5, Finding a Mentor.)

   * List the teachers who are familiar with your topic.

     _____

     _____

     _____

     _____

Make appointments to discuss your project with each teacher and write the time and
date next to the teacher's name. Take a notebook, pen, and your completed
Worksheets 1, 2, and 3 along to each appointment.

   * List the teachers in order of your preference. Consider these questions as you
     compile the list:
     Do I want to work with a teacher I already know?
     Do I think I can develop a working relationship with this teacher?

     _____

     _____

     _____

     _____

Ask your first preference if he or she will serve as your project advisor. Continue
down the list until you find an advisor (remember that teachers may already be
advising other students and may not have time to assist you too).

My Project Advisor is _____
My advisor's office hours (or times when we can meet):

_____

_____

Step 5: Selecting a Mentor

If you need an expert on your topic or if your Independent Project is outside the scope of the school's curriculum, you will probably need to find a mentor. Generally a mentor is defined as a subject area specialist who is able to recommend specific courses of action or specific ways to do a project. Your mentor may be an expert in the community or, perhaps, a relative.

Your mentor will:
- approve your proposal,
- suggest resources,
- consult with you on your plan and progress,
- offer expert advice,
- assist in problem solving, and
- assist in planning your presentation.

If you do not already know an expert on your topic, you may be able to find one by contacting professional organizations in the field that encompasses your topic. You should look in the telephone book and on the Internet for addresses and telephone number or e-mail addresses for such organizations. You may also be able to find possible mentors by asking your project advisor, your parents, or your teachers.

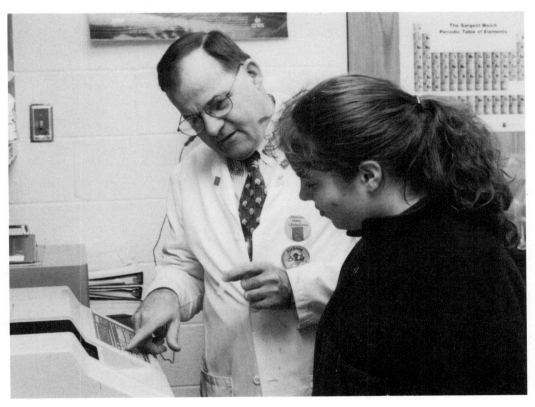

Worksheet 5: Selecting a Mentor

List the names, telephone numbers, addresses, and e-mail addresses of possible mentors suggested by your project advisor, your parents, and your teachers.

- Contacts suggested by your project advisor:

1. name: _____ date contacted:_____
   address: _____
   telephone: _____ e-mail: _____
   notes: _____
   _____

2. name: _____ date contacted:_____
   address: _____
   telephone: _____ e-mail: _____
   notes: _____
   _____

3. name: _____ date contacted:_____
   address: _____
   telephone: _____ e-mail: _____
   notes: _____
   _____

- Contacts suggested by your parents and teachers:

1. name: _____ date contacted:_____
   address: _____
   telephone: _____ e-mail: _____
   notes: _____
   _____

2. name: _____ date contacted:_____
   address: _____
   telephone: _____ e-mail: _____
   notes: _____
   _____

3. name: _____ date contacted:_____
    address: _____
    telephone: _____ e-mail: _____
    notes: _____
    _____

• List the names, addresses, and telephone numbers of professional organizations that encompass your topic:

1. name of organization: _____
    _____ date contacted:_____
    name of contact person: _____
    address: _____
    telephone: _____ e-mail: _____
    notes: _____
    _____
    _____

2. name of organization: _____
    _____ date contacted:_____
    name of contact person: _____
    address: _____
    telephone: _____ e-mail: _____
    notes:_____
    _____
    _____

3. name of organization: _____
    _____ date contacted:_____
    name of contact person: _____
    address: _____
    telephone: _____ e-mail: _____
    notes: _____
    _____
    _____

Write, telephone, or e-mail your request to all the organizations and at least three of the persons suggested above. There is a sample letter on the next page for you to use as a pattern. In the sections above, circle the address or telephone number you used and the date you mailed the letter or made the call.

Sample letter to a mentor:

803 Maple Street
Anytown, PA 17522
October 10, xxxx

Dr. Julius Sumner
University of Anytown
Anytown, PA 17522

Dear Dr. Sumner:

Anytown High School requires each student to complete an Independent Project as a requirement for graduation. I am a junior at Anytown High School and I have elected to complete a project dealing with the unique history of this town through a study of tombstones dating from 1716 to 1850.

My history teacher, Mrs. Virginia Edwards, attended a lecture you presented last year that focused on the epitaphs of gravestones from the nineteenth century. Would you be willing to meet with me to discuss my research? Mrs. Edwards is my project advisor, but she suggested that it would be very beneficial for me to have an expert in the field as my mentor. A mentor's responsibilities are:

- to approve my proposal,
- to suggest resources,
- to consult on my plan and progress,
- to offer expert advice,
- to assist in problem solving, and
- to assist in planning my presentation.

I became interested in this project when I noticed a seemingly large number of children's' gravestones from 1816 in our local cemetery. I would like to research the cause of these deaths and other information that can be gleaned from tombstones. I have done a substantial amount of background reading, but I can see that I will need help in locating further articles and books. I am intrigued by this topic and I hope that you will be willing to discuss my project with me. I can be reached at 225-xxxx after 4 PM or on weekends or by e-mail at 1student@anytown.net. If you would like to speak to my project advisor, Mrs. Virginia Edwards, she can be contacted at the high school (226-xxxx).

Thank you for your time and consideration.

Sincerely,

One Student

Step 6: Constructing a Time Line

You and your project advisor and/or mentor must set up a time line for the completion of your Independent Project. Among the several ways to accomplish this task are:

- a dated list,
- a calendar-type time line, or
- a flowchart.

A time line constructed as a dated list or as a calendar allows you to incorporate holidays, vacations, and weekends into your schedule and allows your advisor and/or mentor to suggest convenient meeting times. Below are examples of a dated list and a calendar-type time line:

A dated list:

Sept. 20	Complete Step 1, Selecting a Topic
Sept. 30	Complete Step 2, Refining the Topic
Oct. 5	Complete Step 3, Developing the Topic into a Project

A calendar-type time line:

Sun	Mon	Tue	Wed	Thu	Fri	Sat
1	2	3	4	5	6	7
8	9	10	11	12	13	14

A flowchart provides a means by which to schedule certain tasks based upon the completion of other parts of your project.

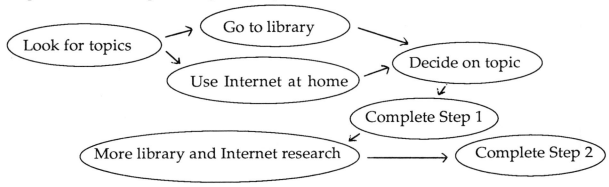

Worksheet 6: Constructing a Time Line

Construct your time line as a dated list or flowchart from the example in Step 6 or the calendar on the next page.

Sun	Mon	Tue	Wed	Thu	Fri	Sat
	1	2	3	4	5	6
7	8	9	10	11	12	13
14	15	16	17	18	19	20
21	22	23	24	25	26	27
28	29	30				

Step 7: Researching Your Topic

You can find information about your topic in the school Media Center, the public library, on the Internet, and directly from experts or others knowledgeable about your topic. Use the library's computer catalog and the Periodic Guide to search for books and magazines about your topic. Browse through the reference section of the library and scan the computer online data bases.

Some sources to try are:
- Magazine Articles Summaries (M.A.S.)
- News Bank
- Biology Digest
- Online Computer Library Center (OCLC)
- Social Issues Resources Series (SIRS)
- SIRS Science

Tape record interviews after requesting permission and keep letters and hard copies of e-mail in a folder.

While reading about your topic, striking statements should be copied exactly, placed within quotation marks, and documented. This will enable you to use them later, if applicable, and give proper credit to the author. Look for unique bits of information that would give you an unusual focus for your project.

Take organized notes in ink and keep them in a loose-leaf notebook or on index cards. Follow the format below or one your advisor provides.

Date:
Article Title:
Author:
Title of Book or Periodical
Publisher and Date of Publication:
Pages:
Useful Material:

Your advisor may suggest following the school's format for listing your references in the bibliography. Many schools use *the Handbook for Writers of Research Papers* published by the Modern Language Association of America (MLA). Below is a generalized bibliographic style:

Books: Author (last name, first name). *Title* (italicize or underline). City of publication: Publisher, date.

Articles: Author (last name, first name). "Title of Article." (in quotations) *Magazine* (italicize or underline) (month day, year): page numbers.

Worksheet 7: Researching Your Topic

Use this worksheet to keep a list of the sources you have used and of the keywords you have used with Internet search engines.

Sources I have checked:

1. _____
2. _____
3. _____
4. _____
5. _____
6. _____
7. _____
8. _____
9. _____
10. _____

Search engines I have tried and key words I have used:
1. _____
   key words _____
   _____
2. _____
   key words _____
   _____
3. _____
   key words _____
   _____
4. _____
   key words _____
   _____
5. _____
   key words _____
   _____
6. _____
   key words _____
   _____

Write the bibliographic entries for references you have found thus far. You will have more to add later as you continue your research. Use the format your advisor gives you or the general format from the previous page.

Step 8: Writing Your Proposal

Most Independent Projects require a written proposal that must be reviewed and approved by teachers or administrators. A proposal form generally includes:
- the purpose or objectives of the project,
- the reason for selection,
- strategies for completion,
- a timeline,
- resources and materials,
- documentation,
- the form of the final product,
- the form of the presentation, and
- evaluation criteria.

Your completed Worksheets provide you with much of the material necessary to write your proposal.

1. The purpose or objectives: The brief statement you will need to explain the value, impact, or importance of what you hope to achieve by completing the project is the same as you wrote on Worksheet 2, item #5.

2. The reason for selection: A statement must be given to explain why you chose your project. You have already written this on Worksheet 3.

3. Strategies for completion: A plan must be stated to explain what data-gathering techniques and procedures you expect to use in order to complete your project. You have already outlined this information on Worksheet 3.

4. A time line: You need to attach a time line for the completion of your Independent Project. You and your advisor and/or mentor will check it periodically as a means of monitoring your progress. The time line should identify specific tasks and their completion dates. You may attach the time line you constructed in Worksheet 6.

5. Resources and materials: A bibliography, which can contain reference materials, CD-ROM, personal interviews, surveys, audio tapes, video tapes, etc. must be provided. You already have your initial bibliography from Worksheet 7.

6. Documentation: Briefly explain how you will document the time you spend working on your Independent Project. Refer to Worksheet 3.

7. The form of final product: The explanation of the end product of your Independent Project is the same as you wrote on Worksheet 3.

8. The form of the presentation: You need to describe the ideas you have for your presentation. You wrote comments for this on Worksheet 3.

9. Evaluation criteria: In many school districts you have the opportunity to determine the criteria by which your Independent Project will be evaluated. The evaluation criteria for the product, the paper, and the presentation may include:
- the thoroughness of literature research,
- the use of organizational skills,
- the validity of the research methods,
- the relevance of the interpretations, and conclusions,
- the originality of the end product,
- the quality of the presentation,
- the demonstration of effective speaking and writing skills.

Use Worksheet 8 for your Independent Project proposal or use the form your advisor provides.

Worksheet 8: Writing Your Proposal

INDEPENDENT PROJECT PROPOSAL

Title: ______________________________

Purpose/Objectives: ______________________________

Reason for Selection: ______________________________

Completion Strategies: ______________________________

Time line: (attach your time line or flowchart)

Resources and Materials: (attach your bibliography)

Form of Final Product: _____

_____

_____

_____

_____

_____

Documentation: _____

_____

Presentation: _____

_____

_____

_____

_____

_____

_____

_____

Evaluation Criteria: _____

_____

_____

_____

_____

_____

_____

Step 9: Writing Your Paper

The paper that accompanies your Independent Project can take several forms. The type of project will dictate whether the paper will be a report or a full-fledged research paper.

You may want to refer to Step 3 for the different types of projects. Your Independent Project may be a combination of types or it may not fit neatly into any of the categories.

Analysis projects generally require a formal research paper like one you might complete for an English or literature class. A science fair project necessitates a formal scientific paper. A generalized format can be found in some of the sources in Appendix B or you may use the guidelines below. Your advisor may want you to write in the style of a scientific journal in your particular field. Exhibition and demonstration projects require less formal reports.

A formal research paper usually includes:

- a title page,
- an abstract or summary,
- an introduction with background information with references to other works cited,
- a research procedure or experimental method,
- a results section (often with tables and graphs),
- an analysis and discussion,
- a conclusion, and
- a bibliography or references section.

A report generally includes:

- a title page,
- the body of the report, and
- a bibliography.

Your paper must explain the background, importance, and impact of your Independent Project and provide supporting information or data. You should make references to the work of others and give them the proper credit in footnotes or endnotes. You will explain the results of your research, how you analyzed those results, and what conclusions you have drawn.

Certain Independent Projects, such as science fair projects and surveys, will require the use of statistics in order to understand the significance of your results. Your advisor, mentor, or mathematics teacher can assist you with the application of statistical analysis.

Worksheet 9: Writing Your Paper

Carefully go over the items in this checklist and attach it to the first draft of your Independent Project paper.

RESEARCH PAPER:

- ☐ a title page,
  - ☐ title
  - ☐ your name
  - ☐ your school
  - ☐ your advisor and/or mentor
  - ☐ date

- ☐ an abstract or summary,

- ☐ an introduction
  - ☐ background information
  - ☐ references to other works cited,

- ☐ a research procedure or experimental method,
  - ☐ clearly stated steps,
  - ☐ materials listed,
  - ☐ sources of techniques listed

- ☐ a results section,
- ☐ an analysis and discussion,
- ☐ a conclusion,
- ☐ a bibliography.

REPORT:

- ☐ a title page,
  - ☐ title
  - ☐ your name
  - ☐ your school
  - ☐ your advisor and/or mentor
  - ☐ date

- ☐ the body of the report,

- ☐ a bibliography.

Step 10: Designing Your Presentation

Your presentation is your opportunity to show what you know. Careful planning and attention to detail are critical.

Review the ideas you wrote for your presentation on Worksheet 3 and consider the ideas you have read about. Below are some examples of different presentations:

- computer slideshow,
- storyboards,
- photograph exhibit,
- audio or video tapes,
- overhead transparencies,
- slide show,
- three-dimensional display,
- charts,
- graphs,
- role-playing,
- architectural design,
- booklet,
- brochure,
- cartoons,
- scrapbook,
- fashion design,
- art display.

Be aware that there may be limited equipment for you to use and that many other students may be making presentations at the same time. Reserve the equipment you need early and be sure to allow time to practice with it. Have backups of all your materials—videotapes, computer disks, transparencies, etc. Consider all the materials and equipment you will need, such as:

- an easel,
- dry erase board, pens, and eraser,
- overhead projector and screen,
- LCD projector and computer,
- VCR and television monitor,
- podium,
- remote control,
- pointer,
- slide projector and screen.

Worksheet 10: Designing Your Presentation

Describe your presentation and list your equipment needs. You may want to attach a sketch of certain aspects of your presentation, as well.

My presentation will be _____

_____

_____

_____

_____

_____

_____

_____

_____

_____

_____

_____

The equipment and supplies I will need are:

_____

_____

_____

_____

Step 11: Making Your Self-Evaluation

Your Independent Project will be judged by a panel of community members, teachers, administrators, or classmates. It is also going to be judged by you! The final step of your project is to make a self-evaluation.

You set certain criteria by which your project was to be evaluated on Worksheet 8 and in your proposal. Now it is time for you to see how well you met these criteria.

In your self-evaluation you will want to discuss what you learned from doing your project and what you learned about your ability:

- to learn new skills,
- to organize,
- to meet deadlines,
- to be creative,
- to communicate, and
- to synthesize new information by yourself.

Worksheet 11: Making Your Self-Evaluation

To help you write your self-evaluation, answer the following:

- How challenging was your project? _____
  _____
  _____
  _____
  _____

- How well did you organize your research? _____
  _____
  _____
  _____
  _____

- Did you learn as much as you expected? _____
  _____
  _____
  _____
  _____

- Did you use effective writing skills in your paper? _____
  _____
  _____
  _____
  _____

- Did your end product effectively apply the knowledge you gained in your research? _____
  _____
  _____
  _____
  _____

- Were you able to acquire the skills needed for your project? _____
  _____
  _____
  _____
  _____

- How effectively did you utilize material or equipment to enhance your presentation? _____

_____

_____

_____

_____

- How well did you organize your presentation? _____

_____

_____

_____

_____

- Did you demonstrate effective speaking skills in your presentation? _____

_____

_____

_____

_____

- Did your project clarify aspects of your career plans? _____

_____

_____

_____

_____

- Did your project meet your expectations? _____

_____

_____

_____

_____

- How could you have improved your project? _____

_____

_____

_____

_____

Did the evaluators understand the value of your project? _____

_____

_____

PART 3

INDEPENDENT PROJECT EXAMPLES

Independent Project Example #1

Worksheet 1: Selecting a Topic

To help you pick a topic for your project, complete the following:

- List 3 things you've always wondered about:
    1. *How people end up in the jobs they have.*

    2. *What it would be like to live in another country.*

    3. *Why there are so many tombstones in the cemetery for children who died in 1816.*

- List 3 things you've always wanted to know more about:
    1. photography

    2. pioneers

    3. diseases

- I love to read about:
    detective stories and murder mysteries

- If you could be someone else for just one day, who would you be?
    Bill Gates

- If you could live in another time, when would it be?
    the pioneer times

Which of these ideas can you picture yourself working on for 4 months or more? You'll have to read a lot about it, do some original research or develop a particular focus, explain it to experts and laypeople; and if you really want to make it a worthwhile experience—*breathe it!*

Choose one of these for your project topic.
    The reason for the children's deaths in 1816

Worksheet 2: Refining Your Topic

Write the topic you have tentatively chosen:
   The reason for so many children's deaths in Lancaster County, Pennsylvania,
   in 1816.

Complete the following about your topic:

- Does one encyclopedia article tell just about everything there is to know about your topic?
   No
   (If the answer is "yes," you should choose another topic.)

- Can you spend an hour a day for several months enjoying your topic?
   Yes
   (If the answer is "no," you should pick another topic.)

- Approximately how many books are in the library on your topic?
   9
   (If the number of books is over 30, you should narrow the scope of your topic.)

- Approximately how many magazine articles are in the library on your topic?
   4
   (If the number of articles is over 50, you should narrow the scope of your topic.)

   I may need to look for information that I could get from tombstones other
   than just the deaths of the children.

Write one sentence to explain the focus of your project.
   What can be learned about the unique history of my town through a study of
tombstones dating from 1716 to 1850.

(If you have difficulty putting the idea for your project into one sentence, consider another way to approach the topic or another aspect of the topic on which to focus. You may need to ask your advisor for assistance.)

Worksheet 3: Developing Your Topic into a Project

Write your topic.

The reason for the children's deaths in 1816 in Lancaster County, Pennsylvania, and other interesting information that can be learned from a study of tombstones from 1716 to 1850.

• Write the purpose; the sentence that explains your project (from Worksheet 2).

What can be learned about the unique history of my town through a study of tombstones dating from 1716 to 1850.

• Give a reason for selection of your topic.

While history has never been my favorite subject in school, I discovered a fascinating mystery in an old cemetery. There were many gravestones for young children that were dated 1816. I decided to research the possible historical reasons for these deaths.

• What do you want to learn about your topic?

What caused the children's deaths in 1816 and other interesting information from the tombstones dated 1716-1850.

• How will you go about learning this?

I will research the history of my town in government documents, published histories, and documents at the Historical Society.

• What sources can you use?

family genealogies, newspapers from the period, church records, and general local history books

• Describe what you will do with the topic that will be make your project unique (an experiment, an unusual comparison or fieldwork).

My fieldwork is unusual. I will be taking information directly from the tombstones and verifying and expanding it with research from books and records.

• How will you document the work you do? (experimental data book, diary, journal)

I will keep a journal with the information from each tombstone and the date I took the notes. I will also take notes from the books, old newspapers, and family histories I read. I will photograph the tombstones of the children and others from various periods (divided into historical intervals: 1716-1750; 1751-1783; 1784-1812; 1813-1850).

• What ideas do you have for your presentation?

I plan to present my project as a slide show or a computer presentation (PowerPoint®, Microsoft) with photographs of the tombstones, highlights of the history of my county and town, and possibly family histories.

Worksheet 6: Constructing a Time Line

Construct your time line as a dated list from the example in Step 6 or use the flowchart below or the calendar on the next page.

Sept. 15	Step 1, select topic
Sept. 20	Step 2, refine topic
Sept. 25	Step 3, develop topic
Sept. 30	Step 4, choose an advisor
Oct. 6	Step 5, find a mentor (make list of possible mentors)
Oct. 8	have 3 phone calls made and 3 letters written to possible mentors
Oct. 12	more letters and phone calls, if needed
Oct. 14	meet with advisor
Oct. 16	Step 6, time line
Oct. 20	meet with mentor
Oct. 23-28	Step 7, research
Oct. 28	order books and articles as interlibrary loans
Nov. 1	Step 9, worksheet for paper and meet with advisor (discuss progress and proposal)
Nov. 2	call mentor (discuss progress and proposal)
Nov. 10	Step 8, proposal
Nov. 11-16	go to local cemeteries to take photos, get books from Historical Society
Nov. 16	take photos to be developed (as slides)
Nov. 17-22	research old newspapers
Nov. 23	pick up photos
Nov. 23-28	(Thanksgiving Vacation)
	meet with mentor to look at slides and discuss progress and presentation ideas
	write a rough draft of paper
Dec. 1	meet with advisor to discuss progress and paper
Dec. 2-8	rewrite paper
Dec. 10	give copies of paper to advisor and mentor
Dec. 11	take more photos, if needed
Dec. 15	Step 10, final design of presentation
Dec. 16	meet with advisor to discuss presentation and changes to paper
Dec. 17	meet with mentor to discuss presentation and changes to paper
Dec. 23-Jan. 2	make final corrections to paper
	rehearse presentation

Jan. 3	reserve library conference room to rehearse presentation with slide projector
Jan. 7	rehearse presentation in library
Jan. 8	rehearse presentation in library with advisor
Jan. 12	rehearse presentation with mentor
Jan. 13-18	rehearse at home (ask to take a slide projector home)
Jan. 21	presentation
Jan. 22	Step 11, self-evaluation
Jan. 30	meet with advisor to discuss self-evaluation and advisor evaluation
Feb. 1	pick up mentor's evaluation and send thank-you note to mentor and advisor

Worksheet 7: Researching Your Project

Use this worksheet to keep a list of the sources you have used and of the keywords you have used with Internet search engines.

Sources I have checked:
1. _Magazine Articles Summaries (M.A.S.)_
2. _News Bank_
3. _Groliers Encyclopedia_
4. _Online Computer Library Center (OCLC)_
5. _Social Issues Resources Series (SIRS)_
6. _Encyclopedia Britannica_
7. _____
8. _____

Search engines I have tried and key words I have used:
1. _Alta Vista_ key words _tombstones; cemeteries_
2. _Excite_ key words _tombstones; graves_
3. _Infoseek_ key words _tombstones; epidemics_
4. _Lycos_ key words _tombstones; cemeteries_
5. _Yahoo_ key words _epidemics (1800s)_
6. _____ key words _____

Write the bibliographic entries for references you have found thus far. You will have more to add later as you continue your research. Use the format your advisor gives you or the general format from the previous page.

A Genealogical Guide to Berk's County Private Cemeteries. Reading, PA: Miller/Lash/Lorah, 1992.

Coffin, Margaret M. _Death in Early America_. New York: Elsevier/Nelson Books, 1976.

Colman, Penny. _Corpses, Coffins, and Crypts: A History of Burial_. New York: Henry Holt and Company, 1997.

Fisher, Charles Adam. _Early Pennsylvania Births, 1675-1875_. Baltimore: Genealogical Pub. Co., 1979.

Patterson, Karl David. _Pandemic Influenza_. Totowa, NJ: Rowman & Littlefield, 1986.

Smith, Elmer L. _Gravestone Designs in Early America_. Applied Arts c1968.

pamphlets from the Historical Society (no publishers, no authors, no dates)
    Tombstone record from the Asbury Cemetery
    Bible records of Martin B. George
    Genealogy Cemetery records

Worksheet 8: Writing Your Proposal

INDEPENDENT PROJECT PROPOSAL

Title: _____ *The 1816 Epidemic* _____

_____

Purpose/Objectives: _____ *The purpose of my Independent Project is to gain a deeper* *understanding of the unique history of my town through a study of tombstones* *dating from 1716 to 1850.* _____

_____

_____

Reason for Selection: _____ *While history has never been my favorite subject in* *school, I discovered a fascinating mystery while wandering through an old* *cemetery. There were many gravemarkers for young children that were dated 1816.* *I decided to research the possible historical reasons for these deaths.* ____

_____

_____

Completion Strategies: _____
_____ *1. photograph the tombstones of the children and others from various* *periods (divided into historical intervals: 1716-1750; 1751-1783; 1784-1812; and 1813-* *1850)* _____
_____ *2. research the history of my town (use government documents, church* *records, published histories, documents from the Historical Society, family* *genealogies, and newspapers from the period)* _____

_____ *3. use this information to attempt to discover the nature of the "epidemic"* *among children in or around 1816* _____

_____

_____

_____

_____

_____

_____

_____

Time line: (attach your time line or flowchart) *see attached*

Resources and Materials: (attach your bibliography) *see attached*

Form of Final Product: *I will have a photograph album of the pictures of the children's tombstones and my paper.*

Documentation: *I will keep a dated journal of my research.*

Presentation: *I plan to present my project as a slide show or computer presentation (PowerPoint, Microsoft) with photographs of the tombstones and an outline of the history of the county and town, and family histories.*

Evaluation Criteria: *1. the thoroughness of the literature search*
2. the validity of the research methods, the interpretations, and conclusions
3. the quality of the paper and the presentation

Worksheet 10: Designing Your Presentation

Describe your presentation and list your equipment needs. You may want to attach a sketch of certain aspects of your presentation, as well.

My presentation will be _a slide presentation of the tombstones of the children. I will also use an overhead projector to show some of the family histories and newspaper accounts of the cases of pneumonia from 1816._

The equipment and supplies I will need are:
slide projector and my slides
remote control for slide projector
screen
overhead projector and my transparencies

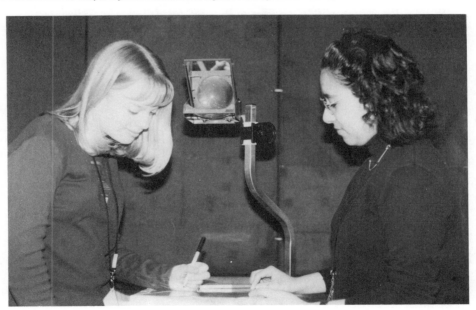

Worksheet 11: Making Your Self-Evaluation

To help you write your self-evaluation, answer the following:

- How challenging was your project? *My Independent Project was challenging for me because I had never done so much research on my own. I also had to discuss what I wanted to learn with adults other than teachers (at the Historical Society and the county courthouse). I was satisfied with the project overall and learned a lot.*

- How well did you organize your research? *This is really the first time I kept organized notes for a report. I used a three-ring binder instead of note cards and I didn't lose anything I needed. My advisor suggested making an outline for my paper before I started writing it and that helped me keep things in a logical order.*

- Did you learn as much as you expected? *Yes. I had hoped to find out why so many children died in 1816 and I learned about an outbreak of pneumonia from the local newspapers from that time. I was even able to find mention of two children who died of pneumonia and I found their tombstones.*

- Did you use effective writing skills in your paper? *Yes. I had to rewrite my paper three times, but my advisor was very pleased with the final copy. My mentor said he will use some of my research in his next talk.*

- Did your end product effectively apply the knowledge you gained in your research? *Yes. I labeled all the photos of the tombstones with as much local and family history as I could find. The photo album was very nice and my mentor wants to use it, too.*

- Were you able to acquire the skills needed for your project? *Yes. But I had to retake some of the photos. I had to learn more about the correct amount of light and shutter speed.*

- How effectively did you utilize material or equipment to enhance your presentation?   *I think the slide show was very effective. The slides were large enough and clear enough for the judges to see the inscriptions easily. My overhead transparencies could have been a little clearer.*

- How well did you organize your presentation?   *Because I practiced so much, my presentation was very well organized. It was pretty easy to remember everything I wanted to say because when I switched to a new slide, it was clear what I was supposed to talk about at that time. I had a list of when I wanted to put up my transparencies. Since I had practiced so much, I also knew that I needed to write that list very large and very dark in order to see it when the lights were out.*

- Did you demonstrate effective speaking skills in your presentation? *Yes, but only because I had practiced so much. My mentor sat in the back and said he would raise his hand if I needed to speak louder. I was pretty comfortable, but a little nervous.*

- Did your project clarify aspects of your career plans?   *No, but I don't hate history so much now.*

- Did your project meet your expectations?   *Actually my Independent Project was a lot more fun to do than I thought it would be.*

- How could you have improved your project?   *I could have gone to more cemeteries or looked for other dates when many people died. I would have liked to have been able to look at cemeteries all over the state and in other areas to see if as many children died there as here. The newspaper accounts said the outbreak of pneumonia was widespread.*

- Did the evaluators understand the value of your project?   *Yes. They asked several logical questions and they asked if I had thought of working for the Historical Society.*

Independent Project Example #2

Worksheet 1: Selecting a Topic

To help you pick a topic for your project, complete the following:

- List 3 things you've always wondered about:
  1. *How naturally colored cotton is different from regular white cotton?*

  2. *How veterinarians are trained?*

  3. *What is the solution to the blue mold infestation that attacks crops in my county?*

- List 3 things you've always wanted to know more about:
  1. *Colored cotton*

  2. *Veterinarians*

  3. *Volkswagens*

- I love to read about:
  science and Volkswagens

- If you could be someone else for just one day, who would you be?
  a veterinarian

- If you could live in another time, when would it be?
  the future

Which of these ideas can you picture yourself working on for 4 months or more? You'll have to read a lot about it, do some original research or develop a particular focus, explain it to experts and laypeople; and if you really want to make it a worthwhile experience—*breathe it!*

Choose one of these for your project topic.
     Naturally colored cotton

Worksheet 2: Refining Your Topic

Write the topic you have tentatively chosen:
Naturally colored cotton

Complete the following about your topic:

• Does one encyclopedia article tell just about everything there is to
 know about your topic?
  _N o_
 (If the answer is "yes," you should choose another topic.)

• Can you spend an hour a day for several months enjoying your topic?
  Yes
 (If the answer is "no," you should pick another topic.)

• Approximately how many books are in the library on your topic?
  None, but there are 12 listed in the university library that I can get through
 interlibrary loans.
 (If the number of books is over 30, you should narrow the scope of your topic.)

• Approximately how many magazine articles are in the library on your topic?
  2, but there are many scientific journal articles that I can get through
 interlibrary loans
 (If the number of articles is over 50, you should narrow the scope of your topic.)

• Write one sentence to explain the focus of your project. _How do the_
 characteristics that affect the quality of cotton fiber compare in naturally colored
 cotton and common white cotton.

(If you have difficulty putting the idea for your project into one sentence, consider
another way to approach the topic or another aspect of the topic on which to focus.
You may need to ask your advisor for assistance.)

Worksheet 3: Developing Your Topic into a Project

Write your topic.

> *A comparison of the fiber characteristics of naturally colored cotton and common white cotton.*

- Write the purpose; the sentence that explains your project (from Worksheet 2).

> *How do the characteristics that affect the quality of cotton fiber (wax content, fineness, maturity, Micronaire rating, and length) compare in naturally colored cotton and common white cotton?*

- Give a reason for selection of your topic.

> *I chose this topic for my Independent Project in order to continue my study of naturally colored cotton that I began in 9th grade. I would like to do chemical analyses on the different cotton samples and try to grow some colored cotton. (My career goal is to become a veterinarian or a plant breeder.)*

- What do you want to learn about your topic?

> *How the quality of cotton fiber is affected by the wax content, fineness, maturity, Micronaire rating, and length.*
>
> *How do these characteristics compare in naturally colored cotton and common white cotton?*

- How will you go about learning this?

> *I will read books and scientific journal articles about naturally colored cotton and the methods for analyzing cotton fiber. I will have to learn how to analyze the fiber.*

- What sources can you use?

> *books and scientific journal articles (from university libraries through interlibrary loans)*
>
> *professional cotton researchers*
>
> *professional cotton growers*

- Describe what you will do with the topic that will be make your project unique (an experiment, an unusual comparison or fieldwork).

> *I will learn how to measure the wax content, fineness, maturity, and length of cotton fiber and I will try to find a professional laboratory to measure the*

Micronaire rating. I will grow naturally colored cotton and common white cotton in a field my aunt has.

• How will you document the work you do? (experimental data book, diary, journal)

I will document my work in a scientific data book/logbook.

• What ideas do you have for your presentation?

I will enter my project in the local and district science fairs and other scientific competitions. These presentations will be a three-dimensional display and/or a PowerPoint (Microsoft) computer presentation.

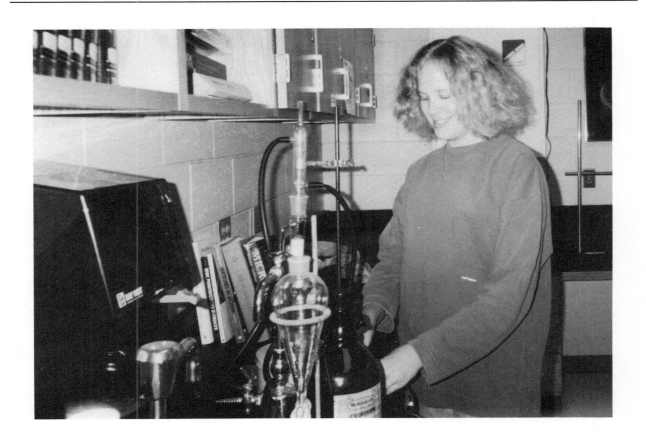

Independent Project Example #2

Worksheet 6: Constructing a Time Line

Construct your time line as a dated list or flowchart from the example in Step 6 or the calendar on the next page.

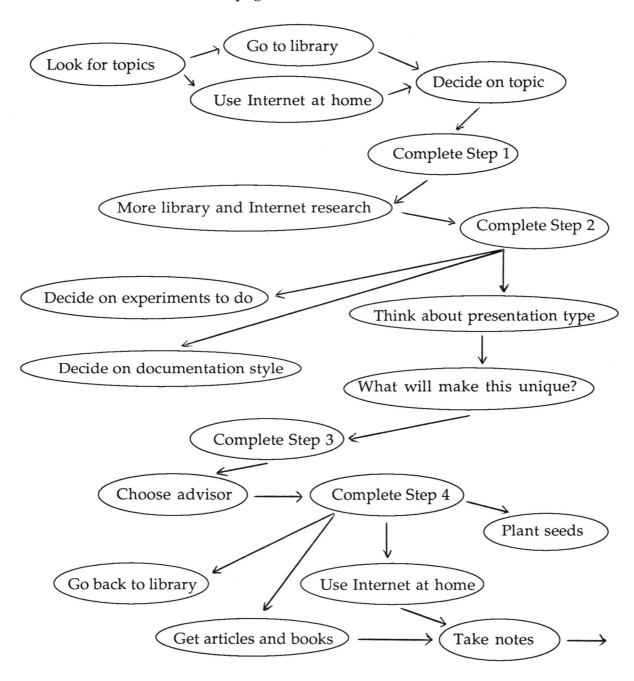

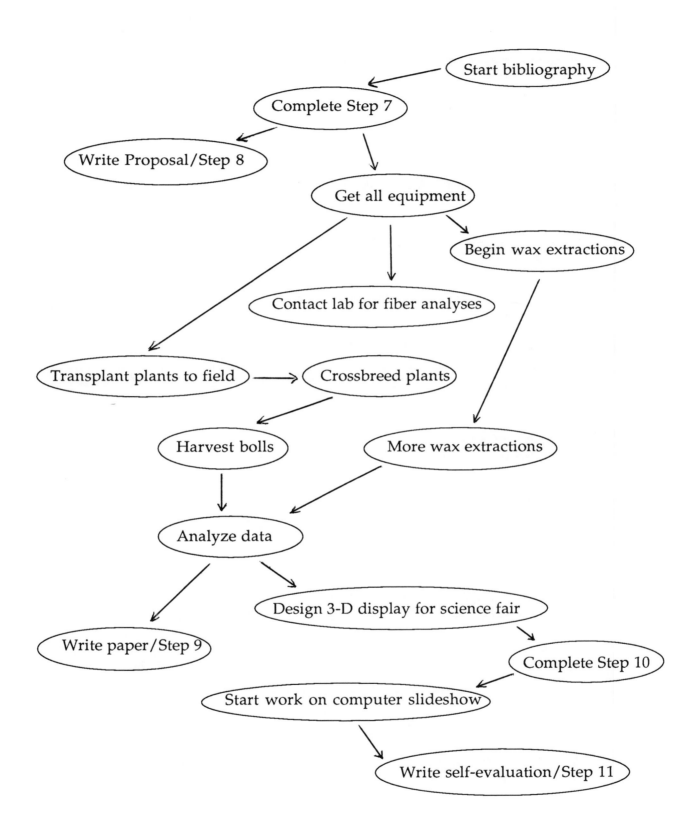

Worksheet 7: Researching Your Project

Use this worksheet to keep a list of the sources you have used and of the keywords you have used with Internet search engines.

Sources I have checked:

1.   *Magazine Articles Summaries (M.A.S.)*
2.   *News Bank*
3.   *Biology Digest*
4.   *Online Computer Library Center (OCLC)*
5.   *SIRS Science*
6.   _____
7.   _____
8.   _____

Search engines I have tried and key words I have used:
1.   *Alta Vista*   key words *naturally colored cotton*
2.   *Excite*   key words *cotton fiber/characteristics*
3.   *Infoseek*   key words *naturally colored cotton*
4.   *Lycos*   key words *cotton fiber/characteristics*
5.   *Yahoo*   key words *naturally colored cotton, cotton*
6.   _____   key words   *fiber tests*

Write the bibliographic entries for references you have found thus far. You will have more to add later as you continue your research. Use the format your advisor gives you or the general format from the previous page.

Note: I have used the format of the scientific journals in my field.

Bell, Thomas M. *The World Of Cotton*. Washington, DC: ContiCotton, EMR, 1989.
Carter, Lark P. and Stephen R. Chapman. *Crop Production: Principles and Practices*. San Francisco, CA: W. H. Freeman and Company, 1976.
Conrad, Carl M., "Determination of Wax in Cotton Fiber; A New Alcohol Extraction Method." *Industrial and Engineering Chemistry*. Dec., 1994, 749-748.
Hamby, Dame S. *The American Cotton Handbook*. New York: Interscience, 1965. Vol. 1 & 2.
Poehlman, John Milton and David Allen Sleper. *Breeding Field Crops*. Ames, Iowa: Iowa State University Press, 1995.
Selsam, Millicent E. *Cotton*. New York: William Morrow and Company, 1982.

Worksheet 8: Writing Your Proposal

INDEPENDENT PROJECT PROPOSAL

Title: _____ *A Comparison of Fiber Characteristics of Naturally Colored Cotton and* _____ *White Cotton.* _____

Purpose/Objectives: _____ *The quality of cotton fiber is affected by the wax content,* _____ *fineness, maturity, Micronaire rating, and length. How do these characteristics* *compare in naturally colored cotton and common white cotton?* _____

Reason for Selection: _____ *I chose this topic for my Independent Project in order to* *continue my study of naturally colored cotton which I began in ninth grade. I had* *no experience in chemistry, so I needed to learn many new skills. I acquired these* *from my advisor. This project relates to one of my possible career goals: a degree in* *agricultural sciences (specifically plant breeding).* _____

Completion Strategies: _____ *Wax Extraction: Extractions will be made with a Soxhlet extractor assembly* *and will be completed by Feb. 1. Each of the six extractions will require four hours,* *after the assembly of the equipment and preparation of the cotton samples.* *Fiber Analyses: Cotton fiber from the field and from samples from Arizona,* *New Mexico, Mississippi, and Louisiana will be measured for fineness, length,* *maturity, and processing quality (Micronaire rating; USDA Laboratory).* *Statistical Analyses: Wax content, measurements of fineness, length,* *maturity, and Micronaire ratings will be statistically analyzed.* *Field Work: Cotton seed from my previous year's field will be planted along* *with new naturally colored cotton seed and common white cotton seed. Plants will* *be raised in a green house for one month and then transplanted to the field. Bolls* *will be harvested and the fiber analyzed.* _____

Time line: (attach your time line or flowchart) *see attached*

Resources and Materials: (attach your bibliography) *see attached*

Form of Final Product: _The product of my Independent Project will be the three-dimensional display of my experimental procedures, results, statistics, and conclusions. I will also have actual samples of the cotton I have grown and the wax extraction assembly._

Documentation: _Experimental notes and research notes will be kept in a logbook._

Presentation: _My Independent Project will be presented at the school and district science fairs and in other scientific competitions. In the science fairs, my presentation will be a research paper, the three-dimensional display, and an oral explanation. In some of the other scientific competitions, my presentation will be on PowerPoint (Microsoft), along with the research paper and an oral presentation._

Evaluation Criteria: _____
_   1. the thoroughness of the literature research;_
_   2. the validity of the experimental methods, analyses, field work, and_
_   conclusions; and_
_   3. the quality of the product and the presentation._
Note: the evaluation will be made by professional scientists who serve as judges in
_ these competitions_

Worksheet 10: Designing Your Presentation

Describe your presentation and list your equipment needs. You may want to attach a sketch of certain aspects of your presentation, as well.

My presentation will be _____

My oral presentation for the science fairs will be made based on a three-dimensional (table-top) display with my research posted on it and my apparatus and cotton samples on the table.

My oral presentation for the other competitions will be made from PowerPoint (Microsoft) screens on a computer.

The equipment and supplies I will need are:

display board, three-sided, wooden frame

computer, LCD projector, screen, and my disks

Worksheet 11: Making Your Self-Evaluation

To help you write your self-evaluation, answer the following:

- How challenging was your project? ___*My Independent Project was very challenging for me because I needed to constantly read to find out new information in order to analyze my results. It was also challenging because I had to learn a lot of chemistry in order to do my project.*___

- How well did you organize your research? ___*My research, both literature research and scientific research, was well organized. I needed to stay on track through the whole process in order to meet all the deadlines, not only for the Independent Project part but also for the science competitions. I kept my research notes from the literature in a three-ring binder and my logbook was invaluable for the experimental research.*___

- Did you learn as much as you expected? ___*I learned more than I expected. In fact, for everything I learned, I found several more things that I needed to learn. I was glad to learn all the chemistry because it will help me when I take a chemistry class this coming year.*___

- Did you use effective writing skills in your paper? ___*Yes. I was able to use the background section of my research paper for an English class assignment and my research paper was accepted for presentation to two professional scientists conventions.*___

- Did your end product effectively apply the knowledge you gained in your research? *Yes. My end product was my exhibit and PowerPoint (Microsoft) presentation. Both of these were based on the knowledge I gained in doing my project.*

- Were you able to acquire the skills needed for your project? ___*Yes and no. I was able to acquire the chemistry skills needed, but I did not successfully apply the skills required to crossbreed my plants. I will have to read more and talk to more plant breeders to learn what I did wrong.*___

- How effectively did you utilize material or equipment to enhance your presentation? _My display boards for the science fairs were very effective and the PowerPoint (Microsoft) were very well received, especially the color photographs of my own cotton plants and bolls that I scanned into the computer presentation._

- How well did you organize your presentation? _Both of my presentation types were well organized into: Abstract, Introduction and Background, Purpose and Hypothesis, Experimental Methods, Results and Statistics, Conclusion, and References._

- Did you demonstrate effective speaking skills in your presentation? _Yes. I was complimented several times on my presentation and I now feel very comfortable speaking to groups._

- Did your project clarify aspects of your career plans? _Definitely. I had thought I wanted to become a veterinarian, but I now know that I am better suited to research work. I discovered that I really enjoy working in plant research and I plan to major in agricultural research in college._

- Did your project meet your expectations? _My Independent Project exceeded my expectations._

- How could you have improved your project? _I need to continue my field work and learn more about crossbreeding cotton plants._

- Did the evaluators understand the value of your project? _The judges of all the competitions seemed to be genuinely interested in my research results._

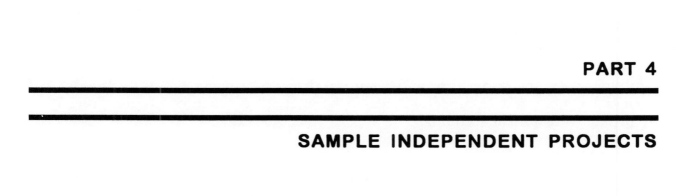

PART 4

SAMPLE INDEPENDENT PROJECTS

Title: Reenacting the Civil War

Content Area: History

BACKGROUND:

1998 was the 135th anniversary of the Battle of Gettysburg and it was "fought" again by thousands of Civil War reenactors. Enthusiasts from all walks of life collect authentic equipment and clothing from the period. Men, women, and children gather at reenactment events and dress in Civil War costumes, both military and civilian. They sleep in period tents, prepare and cook their food in the authentic way, and play period music. Modern-day "sutlers," the merchants who followed the armies, sell Civil War antiques and authentic and reproduction uniforms and equipment for the reenactors and visitors. There are "generals" and "troops" on both the Union and Confederate sides who reenact the battles of the Civil War according to historical accounts.

REFERENCES:

"The Bloodiest Field." Going Places. [television program] June 29, 1998. PBS special (by WNET) (about the Battle of Antietam).

Channing, Steven A. *The Confederate Ordeal; the Southern Home Front.* Alexandria, VA: Time-Life Books, 1989.

Davis, William C. *Rebels & Yankees: The Fighting Men of the Civil War.* New York: Gallery Books, 1989.

Wilkinson, Norman B. *The Brandywine Home Front during the Civil War (1861-1865).* Wilmington, DE: Kaumagraph Co., 1966.

IDEAS FOR DEVELOPMENT:

- a diary of a reenactor—one day in the life of a man or woman
- a video, photographic, or storyboard display of a reenactment
- a complete diagram of several Civil War soldiers with their clothes, equipment, and accoutrements
- a sutler's catalog of equipment, clothing, accessories (eyeglasses, horse gear, etc.)

> **DID YOU KNOW?**
>
> It wasn't just the Blue and the Gray; There was also the Green! One Union unit, Berdan's Sharpshooters, wore green uniforms. Colonel Hiram Berdan selected only the most experienced marksmen and armed them with Sharp's rifles and telescopic sights.

Title: Miniature Trees

Content Areas: Art

Biology

BACKGROUND:

Living sculptures! Bonsai is the art of growing miniature trees in containers. But it is really much more than that: Bonsai in the final result of a variety of disciplines—horticulture, art, and philosophy! A living plant is transferred to a pot so that it continues to live. Evergreen trees, deciduous trees, tropical plants, and all sorts of flowering plants can be used. Copper wires are utilized to bend branches, trunks, and stems to create an artistically shaped plant in a beautiful container. Each bonsai has its own natural beauty, but also the appearance of something else - a forest, a seascape, a cliff. "Where nature and art meet in perfect balance." (Gustafson) These miniaturized trees and plants are seen as "something born of the earth and approaching heaven . . . a piece of the universe with its own life and its own spirit." (Gianfranco)

REFERENCES:

Adams, Peter D. *The Art of Bonsai*. London: Ward Lock, 1992.

Gianfranco, Giorgi. *Simon & Schuster's Guide to Bonsai*. NY: Simon & Schuster, 1990.

Gustafson, Herb L. *Miniature Bonsai*. New York: Sterling Publishing Co., Inc., 1995.

Pessey, Christian. *Bonsai Basics*. New York: Sterling Publishing Co., Inc., 1992.

Stewart, Christine. *Bonsai: A step-by-step guide*. Stanford, CT: Longmeadow Press, 1993.

Student, Shirley. *Beginning Bonsai*. Rutland, VT: C. E. Tuttle, 1993.

IDEAS FOR DEVELOPMENT:

- examples of trees and plants that you have made into bonsai
- a video of the process of creating a bonsai
- drawings of many of the styles or shapes of traditional bonsai
- a storyboard of the evolution of bonsai

DID YOU KNOW?

"Bonsai " means "plant in a container." By 200 AD, Chinese horticulturists could twist the trunks of miniature trees into the calligraphy of the Chinese alphabet.

Title: Photographing the Civil War

Content Areas: Tech. Ed. History

BACKGROUND:

If you look carefully at photographs of Civil War soldiers, you may be able to see the metal brackets that were used to hold the person's head immobile for the 6 seconds it took to expose the picture. Early photographic methods required drastically different materials and skills from our "point-and-click" modern technology. Daguerreotypes, the first practical photographs, were introduced by Louis Daguerre in 1839 and were created by the action of iodine and mercury vapors on a silver-coated copper plate. While much of our Civil War history is recorded in daguerreotypes, a newer format for photographs came into use at that time. Ambrotypes, glass-plate negatives mounted on black backing, were more easily used outdoors.

REFERENCES:

Horan, James David. *Timothy O'Sullivan: America's Forgotten Photographer*. New York: Bonanza Books, 1982.

Hunt, Robert. *Research on Light*. New York: Arno Press, 1979.

Kelbaugh, Ross J. *Introduction to Civil War Photography*. Gettysburg, PA: Thomas Publications. 1991.

Pritzer, Barry. *Matthew Brady*. Greenwich, CT: Brompton Books Corp., 1992.

Thierry, J. *Daguerreotype*. New York: Arno Press, 1979.

IDEAS FOR DEVELOPMENT:

- portfolio of photographs taken and developed with Civil War-era techniques
- a video of the processes used during that era
- diagrams of steps required for each of different photographic techniques
- a computer presentation illustrating the evolution of photographic processes
- construction of a camera obscura

DID YOU KNOW?

The first photograph was taken in France in 1826 by Joseph Neipce with a camera obscura and an 8-hour exposure! The inauguration of a technology that has changed our world began with Neipce's photograph of a building.

Title: The Poetry of Tombstones

Content Areas: English
History
Art

BACKGROUND:

"I told you I was sick!" The inscriptions on old gravemarkers provide a glimpse into the customs and attitudes of the past. Many epitaphs are humorous; many are beautiful. The poetry found on tombstones reflects many of the differences between our modern time and the past. Carved in marble and granite, these inscriptions can move us to laughter and to tears. "Life is a jest, and all things show it;/ I thought so once and now I know it." "A precious one from us has gone/ A voice we loved is still./ A place is vacant in our home/ which never can be filled." "Pray for me, as I will for thee/ That we may meet in Heaven." The customs and traditions of burying the dead differ significantly around the world and over time.

REFERENCES:

Colman, Penny. *Corpses, Coffins and Crypts: a History of Burial.* New York: Henry Holt and Company, 1997.

Fisher, Charles Adam. *Early Pennsylvania Births, 1675-1875.* Baltimore: Genealogical Pub. Co., 1979.

Martin, Douglas D. *Tombstone's Epitaph.* Norman, OK: University of Oklahoma Press, 1997.

Meyer, Richard E., ed. *Cemeteries and Gravemarkers: Voices of American Culture.* Logan, UT: Utah State University Press, 1992.

Smith, Elmer L. *Gravestone Designs.* Lebanon, PA: Applied Arts, 1968.

IDEAS FOR DEVELOPMENT:

- a book of poetry from gravestone inscriptions and analyses of style
- a video or photographic display of old local tombstones
- a display of rubbings from local gravestones
- a study of how tombstone styles and epitaphs reflect the customs of the time and locale

DID YOU KNOW?

The oldest burial sites date to 70,000 BC. The earliest known attempts to artificially create mummies in Egypt date to 2600 BC. The Adena and Hopewell peoples began building burial mounds over 3000 years ago in what is now the Ohio Valley.

Title: On the Home Front

**Content Areas: History
English
Tech. Ed.
Family and Consumer Science**

BACKGROUND:

Americans on the "home front" during World War II were constantly reminded of the war—air raid drills, shortages and rationing, victory gardens, war bonds, and scrap metal drives. Daily life changed in subtle ways. Eggs were still plentiful, but a pound of bacon gobbled up half a week's meat ration stamps; gas couldn't be wasted, so you had to get up an hour early to ride the bus to work; hemlines rose because material was needed for the war; and the best-selling book of 1942 was the *Red Cross First Aid Manual*. Mail from soldiers was censored, news was restricted, and women took all sorts of jobs left open by men going off to war.

REFERENCES:

Abrahamson, James L. *The American Home Front*. Washington, DC: National Defense University Press, 1988.

Bailey, Ronald H. *The Home Front: U.S.A.* World War II. Alexandria, VA: Time-Life Books, Inc., 1977.

Cohen, Stan. *V for Victory: America's Home Front during World War II*. Missoula, MO: Pictorial Histories Publishing Company, Inc., 1991.

Hoopes, Roy. *America Remembers the Home Front.* NY: Watts, 1995.

Noakes, Jerry, ed. *The Civilian in War*. Chicago: Northwestern Univ. Press, 1992.

Reynolds, Clark G. *America at War, 1941-1945: The Home Front*. New York: Gallery Books, 1990.

IDEAS FOR DEVELOPMENT:

- a brochure explaining the role of one of the many agencies (WRA, OPA, OWI)
- a series of posters extolling the virtues of "doing our part" for the war effort
- a storyboard showing what people of all ages did to save and to cope with rationing
- computer presentation of the items to stock an air raid shelter, rules, activities

> **DID YOU KNOW?**
>
> One Illinois boy collected 100 tons of scrap paper for the war drive!
> Only 3 weeks after the government called for scrap drives, U.S. citizens had contributed 5,000,000 tons of pots, pans, horseshoes, car bumpers, and other metal items!

Title: Hyperinstruments

Content Areas: Music
Science
Tech. Ed.

BACKGROUND:

Hyperinstruments are electronically enhanced musical instruments. These are the next-generation interactive instruments and toys such as the "theremin." The theremin, an electronic instrument invented in the early 1900s by Leon Theremin, has become popular in contemporary experimental music circles. It is played by waving one's hands near two metal antennas. One antenna determines the pitch of the sound and the other controls the volume. The theremin and its cousins, the Ondes Martenot and the telharmonium, might remind some listeners of a musical saw. In a less technical sense, the term "hyperinstrument" can mean any new instrument.

REFERENCES:

"Brain Music." *Scientific American Frontiers* (television program), 1998.

Fletcher, Neville H., and Thomas D. Rossig. *The Physics of Musical Instruments*. New York: Springer Verlag, 1998.

Havighurst, Jay. *Making Musical Instruments by Hand*. Gloucester, MA: Rockport Publishing, 1998.

Rothman, Jake. "Simple Theremin Project." *Everyday Practical Electonics* 24, no. 9 (September 1995): 674-678.

www.brainop.media.mit.edu/
www.nashville.net/~theremin

IDEAS FOR DEVELOPMENT:

- construct several homemade hyper-instruments and play them
- electronically analyze the characteristics of the sound of homemade hyperinstruments
- compose a musical selection with a mix of traditional and homemade instruments
- a computer presentation of music composed of sound clips from Internet sites

---

DID YOU KNOW?

A team of researchers at the Massachusetts Institute of Technology has invented a "musical jacket" that is played by touching different parts of its embroidery.

Title: The Development of Military Rations

Content Areas: History
Business
Family and Consumer Science
Tech. Ed.

BACKGROUND:

"An army travels on its stomach." Military leaders since the beginning of organized warfare knew that the ability of soldiers to fight was related to the way they were fed and that often determined victory or defeat. A ration is defined as the allowance of food for the subsistence of one person for one day. In Napoleon's time (until 1810), soldiers usually had to forage for whatever they could find. Civil War soldiers had hardtack, pemmice, jerked beef, flour, and pinole when available. Armies in WW I had 3 basic rations; the standard ration, the trench ration, and the Iron ration. Due to the increased mobility of troops during WW II, many new types of rations were needed: K, D, E, 5-in-1, Assault, Jungle, Parachute, Life raft, etc.

REFERENCES:

Keller, Franz A. *Special Rations for the Armed Forces.* Washington DC: Historical Branch and Office of the Quartermaster General, 1958.*

Marriott, Bernadette M., ed. *Food Components to Enhance Performance.* Washington, DC: National Academy Press, 1994.

Marriott, Bernadette M., ed. *Not Eating Enough.* Washington, DC: National Academy Press, 1995.

The Development of Special Rations for the Army. QMC Historical Studies. Washington, DC: Historical Branch, nd.*

*Available from George A. Petersen, National Capital Historical Sales Inc., P.O. Box 6-5, Springfield, VA 22150 (703-569-6663; fax 703-455-5256)

IDEAS FOR DEVELOPMENT:

- posters comparing the standard rations of various military eras or countries
- a computer presentation of the caloric and nutritional content of various rations
- a storyboard of requirements for rations (stability, cost, appeal, variety, package)
- an analysis of specialty rations (lifeboat rations, pilot's emergency rations, MREs)

DID YOU KNOW?

To solve his army's food problems in 1810, Napoleon Bonapart enlisted the help of Nicholas Appert, a champagne bottler and cook, who developed a method of sealing food in champagne bottles and putting them in boiling water. He had discovered what would only be verified 1/2 a century later— heat-sterilized food!

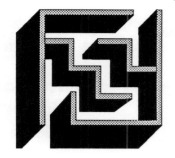

Title: Amazing Mazes

Content Areas: Mathematics
Art

BACKGROUND:

Mazes and labyrinths, confusing intricate networks of passages, date back 4,000 years. The earliest were entirely unicursal labyrinths consisting of a single convoluted path without junctions. These labyrinths were not puzzles, but were used for ritual walking and processions. There were labyrinth motifs in mosaic pavements throughout the Roman Empire, in ancient stone paths in Scandinavia, and in medieval cathedral pavements. Turf mazes in England date back to the Dark Ages. Puzzle hedge mazes became an amusement for kings and princes all over Europe during the 1700s and are still seen in Europe. Today we enjoy mazes in puzzle books or marble toys. Since 1993, Don Frantz has been building mazes in cornfields all over the country. These "living puzzles" have become the latest fad in outdoor entertainment and are made by cutting paths through the corn in patterns such as the Liberty Bell, the Erie Canal, the Statue of Liberty, and a lighthouse.

REFERENCES:

Dobb, Penelope Reed. *The Idea of the Labyrinth: From Classical Antiquity through the Middle Ages.* Ithaca, NY: Cornell University Press, 1992.

Evans, Larry. *3-Dimensional Maze Art.* San Francisco: Troubador, 1980.

Fisher, Adrian. *Secrets of the Maze.* Hauppauge, NY: Barron's Education Series, 1997.

Matthews, William Henry. *Mazes and Labyrinths: Their History and Development.* New York: Dover Publications, 1985.

IDEAS FOR DEVELOPMENT:

- design a unique "living" maze and a grid to transfer it to an actual field
- a computer presentation of the history of mazes
- design a maze to represent the history of your town or state
- construct a rat/mouse maze with moveable dividers for use in the biology department

DID YOU KNOW?

In Greek mythology the Minotaur lived in the Cretan labyrinth and was fed Athenian youths and maidens until it was slain by Thesus who used Ariadne's thread to navigate the maze. The 7-ring design of this labyrinth decorated the coins of Crete from the first century BC.

Title: Victory Gardens

Content Areas: Science
History

BACKGROUND:

Citizens on the home front during World War II were anxious to do their part to help the war effort. To alleviate the labor shortage, supplement rationing, and release food supplies for shipment overseas, many families set out vegetable gardens called "victory gardens." The idea for these backyard and vacant lot gardens dated back to World War I when there was a worldwide food shortage. By 1943 over 20 million victory gardens were producing 40% of all the vegetables grown in the United States. City dwellers planted kitchen crops on the fringe of the sidewalk and on rooftops. Victory gardens also changed dietary habits, and Americans, especially, discovered "new" vegetables such as Swiss chard and kohlrabi.

REFERENCES:

Dotz, Walter L. *All about Vegetables*. San Ramon, CA: Ortho Books, 1990.

Pallotta, Jerry. *The Victory Garden Alphabet Book*. Watertown, MA: Charlesbridge, 1992.

Punch, Walter T., ed. *Keeping Eden: A History of Gardening in America*. Boston: Bulfinch Press, 1992.

Rondale, Robert. *The Encyclopedia of Organic Gardening*. Emmaus, PA: Rodale Publishing, 1992.

Tucker, David M. *Kitchen Gardening in America: A History*. Ames: Iowa State University Press, 1993.

IDEAS FOR DEVELOPMENT:

- a recipe book using the products of victory gardens
- a display of layouts to grow the most on a small or irregular plot
- a bulletin board explaining the varieties (cultivars) of vegetables grown, growth requirements, germination time, time until harvest
- a computer presentation of period slogans, posters, brochures, and newspaper articles

---

DID YOU KNOW?

Even public grounds were used for victory gardens. There were vegetable plots on the lawn of San Francisco's City Hall, in the Boston Commons, at the Portland, OR, zoo, in a New Orleans downtown parking lot, and even on Wilshire Blvd. in L.A.

Title: The Pennsylvania Dutch

Content Areas: English
History
Art

BACKGROUND:

As a result of William Penn's "experiment" in religious tolerance, many Amish settled in Lancaster County, PA, during the 1720s and have attempted to preserve the elements of late 17th-century European rural life by rejecting most of the developments of modern society. The Amish drive horse-drawn buggies, plow fields with teams of mules, do not use electricity, dress in plain dark clothing, and speak unique German dialects. Rather than take unemployment or welfare, they maintain mutual aid funds and help other members with cooperative work such as barn-raisings. There are more than 30,000 Amish in 21 states. with the greatest populations in Pennsylvania, Indiana, and Wisconsin.

REFERENCES:

Kopp, Achim. *The Phonology of Pennsylvania German English.* Susquehanna, PA: Susquehanna University Press, 1999.

Kuhns, Oscar. *German and Swiss Settlement of Colonial PA.* New York: Heritage Books, 1997.

Lester, W. J., W. J. Seifert, and Mark L. Louden. *Word Atlas of Pennsylvania German.* University of Wisconsin Press, 1999.

Reimensnyder, Barbara. *Powpowing in Union County: A Study of Pennsylvania German Folk Medicine.* New York: AMS Press, 1989.

Strassburger, Ralph B., ed. *Pennsylvania German Pioneers.* Camden, ME: Picton Press, 1992.

IDEAS FOR DEVELOPMENT:

make and display examples of Amish folk art (frakturs, distelfinks, quilts, and hex signs)

- learn to prepare some Amish foods and teach them to a middle school class
- a dictionary of Pennsylvania Dutch terms and equivalents in English and German
- a photographic display of Amish artifacts, tools, etc. with names in the dialect

DID YOU KNOW?

Some Amish foods are Shoo-fly pie, (a molasses breakfast pie), scrapple (hog's head), hassenpfeffer (rabbit), Fastnachts (doughnuts for Shrove Tuesday), parshing ponakucka (peach fritters), and gaenseklein (fricasseed goose).

Title: Civil War Medicine

Content Areas: History
Science

BACKGROUND:

At the outbreak of the Civil War the Union army had only 30 surgeons and 84 assistant surgeons. Civilian doctors, "Contract Surgeons," were hired as needed, volunteer regiments brought their own doctors, and a corps of medical students was enlisted as wound-dressers and ambulance attendants. The civilian Hospital Corps was created in 1862 and the Ambulance Corps was authorized in 1864. Civilian Sanitary Commissions provided help in some areas. The Civil War was fought at the end of the medical "Middle Ages"—doctors knew nothing of what caused disease, did not understand the need for sanitation or sterile conditions, and did not know how to halt infection. Chloroform and ether were used as anesthetics, the most common surgical procedure was amputation, and strychnine, mercury compounds, opium, and medicinal whisky were standard remedies.

REFERENCES:

Adams, George Worthington. *Doctors in Blue*. Baton Rouge, LA: Louisiana State Univ., 1996.

Denny, Robert E. *Civil War Medicine*. New York: Sterling Publications, 1995.

Freemon, Frank R. *Gangrene and Glory*. Rutherford, NJ: Fairleigh Dickinson University Press, 1998.

Ropes, Hannah. *Civil War Nurse: The Diary and Letters of Hannah Ropes*. Knoxville, TN: University of Tennessee Press, 1993.

Wilber, C. Keith. *Civil War Medicine 1861 -1865*. NY: Chelsea House Pub., 1999.

IDEAS FOR DEVELOPMENT:

- a study of the diseases, treatment of the period, and the modern treatment
- a diary to describe conditions in Civil War hospitals or prisoner-of-war camps
- a photographic display of medical equipment
- a study of medical training of the time
- create posters, brochures, articles in support of the Sanitary Commissions

---

DID YOU KNOW?

Of the 618,000 deaths on both sides during the Civil War, 66% were the result of disease. Soldiers died from typhoid, dysentery, scurvy, diarrhea, small pox, measles, malaria, scarlet fever, diphtheria, and pneumonia.

Title: Advertising

Content Areas: English
History
Science
Art

BACKGROUND:

"Who's *not* selling something?" There is a science to marketing and advertising products. Manipulation of emotions, symbols, images, and words is the key to good advertising. Products are sold by making customers "need" them and feel insecure without them. The techniques employed include strategic placement of goods (candy and popular cereals placed at children's' eye level in grocery store aisles; bread, milk, and other staples are placed as far apart as possible), subliminal advertising, symbols and logos, and other Madison Avenue "mental engineering" methods. The classic Coca Cola logo is the most widely recognized symbol in the world. Today's advertising strategies must encompass political advertising, the teen-age market, the baby-boomers, and the Internet.

REFERENCES:

Avery, Jim. *Advertising Campaign Planning*. Chicago: Copy Workshop, 1993.
Avery, Jim. *Advertising Campaign Strategy*. Chicago: Copy Workshop, 1997.
Fearon, Robert. *Advertising That Works*. Chicago: Probus Pub. Co., 1991.
Hammeroff, Eugene J., and Herbert S. Gardner, Jr. *The Advertising Agency Business*. Lincolnwood, IL: NTC Business Books, 1997.
Moriarty, Sandra, and Tom Duncan. *Creating and Delivering Winning Advertising and Marketing Presentation*. Lincolnwood, IL: NTC Publication Group, 1996.

IDEAS FOR DEVELOPMENT:

- create new product photo layouts for magazines in several styles
- a computer presentation of marketing techniques used in grocery stores
- a storyboard of advertising techniques aimed at teen consumers
- an analysis of classic advertising
- a videotape of various styles of TV commercials

DID YOU KNOW?

Visual advertisements often make use of an interesting geometric relationship, the Golden Rectangle. Based on the Golden Ratio of 0.618 to 1, Golden Rectangles have been shown to have the most visually pleasing ratio of width to length.

Title: The Art of Museum Display

Content Areas: Art
History
Tech. Ed.

BACKGROUND:

There are museums for just about everything in the world! A museum is defined as an institution devoted to the procurement, care, study, and display of objects of lasting interest or value. Some of the most famous museums are the Louvre, the Metropolitan Museum of Art, and the Smithsonian. The Smithsonian Institution includes 16 museums and galleries, the National Zoo, and numerous research facilities and houses 140 million artifacts and specimens. How are all these items acquired and stored? How are they selected, cared for, and displayed? What decisions must be made when designing museum displays? What are the design strategies for traveling exhibits? Even the most impressive artifacts fail to captivate the viewer unless displayed in a manner that makes them compelling.

REFERENCES:

Danilov, Victor J. *Museum Careers and Training*. Westport, CT: Greenwood Press, 1994.

Karp, Ivan, and Steven D. Lavine, eds. *Exhibiting Cultures*. Washington, DC: Smithsonian Institution Press, 1991.

Kurin, Richard. *Reflections of a Culture Broker: A View of the Smithsonian*. Washington, DC: Smithsonian Institution Press, 1997.

Neal, Arminta. *Help for the Small Museum*. Boulder, CO: Pruett Pub. Co., 1987.

Sixsmith, Mike, ed. *Touring Exhibitions*. Oxford: Butterworth-Heinemann, 1995.

IDEAS FOR DEVELOPMENT:

- a design of an exhibit room made with photos of artifacts from the Internet
- a video of various local museums and an analysis of improvements in the displays
- create a museum of objects in the school
- a manual of museum lighting techniques

DID YOU KNOW?

Some of the oddest museums:
The International Museum of Toilets,
the Voodoo Museum,
the Museum of Questionable Medical Devices,
the Kooks Museum,
the Museum of Bad Art,
the Banana Museum,
and the Museum of Unnatural History!

Title: Women in World War II

**Content Areas: History
English**

BACKGROUND:

"If you can drive a car, you can run a machine." This was one slogan used to reassure some of the 6 million women who entered the workforce during World War II. Women learned to drive steam rollers, operate giant construction cranes, assemble aircraft, and become "lumberjills." They served as Civil Defense workers, airplane spotters, and in the USO, the Women's Land Army, and the Red Cross. In 1942, the government finally officially accepted women into the military—in the WAAC (the largest women's services with 143,000 women),WOWs, WAFS, SPARS, WAVES, Marine Corps Women's Reserve, WASPs, and the British WRENS.

REFERENCES:

Cole, Jean Hascall. *Women Pilots of World War II*. Salt Lake City: University of Utah Press, 1992.

Kein, Albert N. *The CPS Story: An Illustrated History of Civilian Public Service*. Intercourse, PA: Good Books, 1990.

Klein, Yvonne, ed. *Beyond the Home Front: Women's Autobiographical Writing of the Two World Wars.* New York: New York University Press, 1997.

Noggle, Anne. *For God, Country, and the Thrill of It*. Austin: Texas A&M University Press, 1990.

Simmott, Susan. *American Women on the Home Front during WW II*. New York: Franklin Watts, Inc., 1995.

IDEAS FOR DEVELOPMENT:

- a scrapbook of facsimile souvenirs and letters of a woman in the armed services in WW II

- a computer presentation of photos of women in various "men's jobs" during the war

- a study of the societal changes brought about by women entering the workforce

- a bulletin board of the women's armed forces groups, their insignia, uniforms, duties

---

DID YOU KNOW?

Military photographers were sent to factories to get morale-boosting images for the soldiers overseas. On one such assignment, the photographer spotlighted Norma Jean Baker working in an airplane factory and ran her pictures in the Army magazine, *Yank*.

Title: The Engineering of Pyramids

Content Areas: Science
History
Art
Tech. Ed.

BACKGROUND:

　　Pyramids were built by various cultures to serve different purposes. The Assyrians, Sumerians, Nubians, Babylonians, Romans, Javanese, Burmese, Egyptians, Incas, Toltecs, and Mayans all constructed pyramids. Some pyramids were constructed as burial places for kings and pharaohs; some were built as platforms to elevate temples; and most were erected for astronomical purposes. The earliest pyramids were step pyramids such as the Djoser Pyramid at Saqqara; later pyramids were straight-sided like the Great Pyramid at Giza. Pyramid designers were mathematicians and astronomers. The stars were used to fix the exact position of the sides which always face the four points of the compass. Some were constructed of mud bricks (adobe); some of huge blocks of stone. The actual methods by which ancient peoples were able to move the stone blocks is still unknown.

REFERENCES:

　　David, A. Rosalie. *The Pyramid Builders of Ancient Egypt.* Boston: Routledge & K. Paul, 1996.

　　"Great Pyramids." [videorecording] A & E Home Video, 1976.

　　Martell, Hazel. *The Great Pyramid.* Austin, TX: Raintree Steck-Vaughn. 1998.

　　Stewart, Basil. *The Great Pyramid.* New York: ECA Associates, 1993.

　　Stierlin, Henri. *The Maya: Palaces and Pyramids.* Cologne: Taschen American, 1997.

IDEAS FOR DEVELOPMENT:

- a storyboard of theories of the construction of pyramids
- a series of models of various types of pyramids from different countries
- a computer presentation of artifacts, artwork, and pottery from pyramids
- a reconstruction of life in the time of the pyramid construction

---

DID YOU KNOW?

Chichén Itzá, a Mayan pyramid built about 1,600 years ago and built over by the Toltecs in AD 1100, was "discovered" in the jungles of the Yucatán in 1904. Built to elevate a temple and serve astronomical purposes, the pyramid has 365 steps to symbolize the length of a year.

Title: Wedding Customs around the World

Content Areas: Social Studies
Family and Consumer Science

BACKGROUND:

Many Western wedding traditions can be traced back to the days when men stole their wives from neighboring tribes or clans. The honeymoon was the period following the abduction when the groom would go into hiding with his new "bride" so that by the time her family found them she would already be pregnant. By tradition, the groom stands on the bride's right—to keep his sword hand free to fight off her family. Many other traditions originated from the custom of buying a wife. The "bride price" is reflected in tying old shoes to the bridal car, to the word "wedding," and the dowry. Some customs are more modern, such as bridal showers which originated in the 1890s. Tiny gifts were placed inside an umbrella and when it was opened over the bride-to-be, they showered down on her.

REFERENCES:

Allen, Kimberly Burton. *Wedding Wonders*. Glendale Heights, IL: Great Quotations, 1996.

Compton, Anita. *Marriage Customs*. New York: Thomson Learning, 1993.

Gelber, Carol. *Love and Marriage around the World*. Brookfield, CT: Millbrook Press, 1998.

Lee, Vera. *Something Old, Something New: What You Didn't Know About Wedding Customs*. Napierville, IL: Sourcebooks, 1994.

Tegg, William. *The Knot Tied: Marriage Ceremonies of all Nations*. Detroit: Omnigraphics, 1998.

IDEAS FOR DEVELOPMENT:

- a storyboard to compare wedding customs of several cultures
- a display of photos and traditions from weddings of different generations
- a video of traditional wedding foods from different cultures
- a wedding plan that is a composite of the customs of many cultures

DID YOU KNOW?

Amish couples in Pennsylvania announce their wedding intentions in late October. Marriages take place on Tuesdays or Thursdays in November when the crops have all been harvested. The bride's dress is blue or purple and she will be buried in it when she dies.

Title: Castle Construction

Content Areas: History
Tech. Ed.
Art
Family and Consumer Science

BACKGROUND:

The "great age of castles" began nearly 1,000 years ago and lasted for nearly 500 years. Over 15,000 castle were built primarily as fortresses to control and defend large areas in Europe and the Near East during this time (in Spain, Sicily, Syria, Scotland, Wales, Germany, France, England primarily). The earliest known French castle (*Doué-la-Fontaine* in Anjou) was completed in 950 AD. Early castle were made of wood and stood on a mound called a motte. Later, stone was used and large castles, such as Beaumaris in North Wales, required 2,000 laborers and 400 stone masons to complete. Walls were 6 to 16 feet thick and contained structures for defense (hourds, merlons, crenels, machicolations, barbicans, and towers). Scores of grooms, ladies-in-waiting, falconers, knights, pages, pantlers, butlers and others worked inside the medieval castle. Later castles were built to be palaces more than fortresses.

REFERENCES:

Kenyon, John R. *Medieval Fortifications.* New York: St. Martin's Press, 1990.
Nardo, Don. *The Medieval Castle.* San Diego, CA: Lucent Books, 1998.
Oggins, Robin S. *Castles and Fortresses.*
New York: Metrobooks, 1995.
Taylor, A. J. *Studies in Castles and Castle-Building.* London: Hambledon Press, 1986.
Unstead, R. J. *See Inside a Castle.* London: Grisewood and Dempsey, 1986.

IDEAS FOR DEVELOPMENT:

- a display of models of castles from different periods or countries
- a storyboard depicting the life inside a medieval castle
- a computer presentation of the various crafts and skills needed to build a castle
- a display explaining the function of the different parts of a castle
- an illustrated time line of the development of castle types and structures

DID YOU KNOW?

The Neuschwanstein castle in Germany, built for Bavarian King Ludwig II in the 1800s, was the model for the castle at Disneyland and the movie "Sleeping Beauty." It reflects the romanticism of the time and Ludwig's fixation on swans with its swan lake and boats, manmade cave, and forced-air central heating.

Title: Sister Cities

Content Areas: Social Studies
History
Foreign Language

BACKGROUND:

In 1956 President Dwight D. Eisenhower announced "The Sister Cities Program is an important resource to the negotiations of governments in letting the people themselves give expression of their common desire for friendship, goodwill, and cooperation for a better world for all!" Since then, over 1,200 American cities, counties, and states have become partners with cities in 125 countries around the world. Sister Cities International sponsors youth and teacher exchanges, newsletters, scholarships, and awards. Many Sister Cities work on 5-year projects to increase economic development and trade. Does your town have a Sister City? If so, make this unique relationship a part of your school. If your town does not have a Sister City, here is your chance!

REFERENCES:

Burger, Leslie. *Sister Cities*. Minneapolis: Lerner Publications, 1996.

Chilsen, Liz, and Sheldon Rampton. *Friends in Deed: The Story of US - Nicaragua Sister Cities*. Madison, WI: Wisconsin Coordinating Council, 1989.

Lappin, Ben W. *Distant Partners*. Lanham, MD: University Press of America, 1990.

Rickards, Robert C.. *Managing the Metropolis in Japan and Texas: Sister City Relationships, Municipal Finance, and Urban Economic Development Projects*. Austin, TX: LBJ School Press, 1991.

IDEAS FOR DEVELOPMENT:

- develop a complete plan to get a Sister City for your town
- a video done in the two languages of the history of each city (and send a copy to your Sister City)
- a photograph album of unique places and events in your town (with translations) to send to your Sister City

DID YOU KNOW?

Your city or town can get a "Sister City." Hundreds of cities in countries all over the world are waiting to be selected. Countries on the waiting list include Argentina, Austria, Congo, Cypress, Estonia, Montenegro, Madagascar, Mozambique, and Paraguay.

Title: The History of Your Town

Content Areas: History
English
Business

BACKGROUND:
Towns and cities evolve over time. Many of the businesses that thrived in the downtown area in the past no longer exist or have moved to industrial parks or shopping centers. Even residential areas change as people move out to the suburbs. Old photographs in trunks in the attic may have the address of the photographic studio on the back. You might be surprised to find something entirely different at that location now. The archives of the local newspaper should have many photographs of what your town used to look like and advertisements from many old businesses. The historical society will also have information about what your town was like a hundred years ago.

REFERENCES:
Francaviglia, Richard, and Wayne Franklin. *Main Street Revisited.* Iowa City: University of Iowa Press, 1996.

Jakle, John A. *The American Small Town.* Hamden, CT: Archon Books, 1982.

Monkkonen, Eric H. *America Becomes Urban: The Development of U.S. Cities and Towns 1780-1980.* Berkeley: University of California Press, 1990.

Rishel, Joseph F., ed. *American Cities and Towns.* Pittsburgh, PA: Duquesne University Press, 1992.

Ross, Pat. *Remembering Main Street: An American Album.* New York: Viking Studio Books, 1994.

IDEAS FOR DEVELOPMENT:
- a storyboard to show the development of your town over the last century
- a time line of before-and-after photos of the businesses in your town (use the news-paper archives for old photos)
- an analysis of the changes caused by street realignment and new developments
- a booklet of the changes in town government, zoning, agricultural preserves, etc.

DID YOU KNOW?

Even the names of cities and countries change! Columbia, PA, changed its name from Wright's Ferry in the 1780s to try to become the nation's capital; Sri Lanka used to be Ceylon; Iran used to be Persia; Myanmar used to be Burma and its capital, Yangon, used to be Rangoon.

Title: Shipwrecks

Content Areas: History
Science
Art
Tech. Ed.
Business

BACKGROUND:

In 1641 the Spanish galleon, *La Nuestra Señora de la Pura y Limpia Concepción*, sank off the coast of what is now the Dominican Republic with 500 passengers and crew and tons of Mexican silver (bars and newly minted coins). Part of its cargo was recovered in 1687 and the remainder lay hidden until 1978. Exploration of ancient shipwrecks increases understanding of ancient cultures and ways of life. The silver and gold bars and jewelry often make the news, but the nautical equipment (such as astrolabes), musical instruments, games, tools, and bits of daily life help modern people understand the life of those times.

REFERENCES:

Farb, Roderick M. *Diving the Graveyard of the Atlantic.* Birmingham, AL: Menasha Ridge Press, 1991.

Kinder, Gary. *Ship of Gold in the Deep Blue Sea.* New York: Grove/Atlantic, 1998.

Marx, Robert F., and Jenifer Marx. *The Search for Sunken Treasure: Exploring the World's Great Shipwrecks.* Toronto: Key Porter Books, 1996.

Marx, Robert, Jenifer Marx, and Jennifer Marx. *New World Shipwrecks 1492-1825.* Dallas, TX: Ram Pub. Co., 1994.

Thompson, Tommy. *America's Lost Treasures.* New York: Atlantic Monthly Press, 1998.

IDEAS FOR DEVELOPMENT:

- a computer presentation of items salvaged from a shipwreck (photos from Internet sites)
- an account of the research, costs, and skills required for finding and salvaging a shipwreck
- a storyboard of the lifestyle of the period reconstructed from the artifacts found in a shipwreck
- a series of maps detailing the causes of various shipwrecks

> **DID YOU KNOW?**
>
> Pieces of Eight are old silver Spanish coins. Their denomination is 8 *reales*; so they were referred to as "a piece of 8 *reales*." Pieces of Eight were about 93% silver and weighed one Spanish ounce. In the 17th century a sailor earned two Pieces of Eight for a month's work.

Title: Solutions to Prison Overcrowding

Content Area: Social Studies

BACKGROUND:

Prisons of one sort or another have probably been around since civilization began. Punishment of wrong-doers has taken the form of pillories, branding, and confinement within a stockade. In some other countries imprisonment may be very inhumane and in some places the inmates must pay for their food and bedding. As society places more and more criminals behind bars, prisons become more and more overcrowded. What are the solutions? Early parole? Halfway houses? Privatization of prisons? Groups and programs such as Corporal Alternative Sentencing (CAS), Citizens for Effective Justice (CFEJ), and Parole Older Prisoners (POP) attempt to develop workable solutions.

REFERENCES:

McDonald, Douglas C., ed. *Private Prisons and the Public Interest*. New Brunswick: Rutgers University Press, 1990.

Monuments to Failure [videorecording]. Alexandria, VA: PBS Video, 1987.

Paulus, Paul B. *Prison Crowding: A Psychological Perspective*. New York: Springer-Verlag, 1988.

Quinlan, J. Michael. *From Arizona to South Carolina: Transfer of a Prison Design Model*. Washington, DC: U.S. Department of Justice, 1990.

Tonry, Michael, and Kathleen Hatlestad, eds. *Sentencing Reforms in Overcrowded Times*. Oxford: Oxford University Press, 1997.

IDEAS FOR DEVELOPMENT:

- a time line to show the changes in prison populations compared to sentencing changes
- a computer presentation to explain the effects of various solutions
- an analysis of the cost effectiveness of prison privatization
- a study of how overcrowding affects inmates, recidivism rates, and crime within prisons

> **DID YOU KNOW?**
>
> Alcatraz may be the best known prison in the U. S. Built on an island in San Francisco Bay, 1,545 prisoners did time there between 1934 and 1963. Some of the most notorious were Al Capone; Machine Gun Kelly; and "The Birdman of Alcatraz," who never kept birds while in Alcatraz!

Title: Gestures and Different Cultures

Content Areas: Social Studies
History
Family and Consumer Science

BACKGROUND:

There is a language that exists beyond words—the language of the body and its gestures. What impact do these silent forms of communication that may be unconscious have on others' perceptions of us? Nonverbal communication includes eye contact, the direction of gaze, facial expressions, head movements, posture, orientation, and proximity. How do the messages conveyed by gestures and body language differ around the world, how do they affect our interactions with others, and how do they translate into accepted etiquette and social customs and behavior?

REFERENCES:

Axtell, Roger E., and Mike Fornwald. *The Do's and Taboos of Gestures and Body Language around the World*. New York: John Wiley & Sons, 1997.

Morris, Desmond. *Bodytalk: The Meaning of Human Gestures*. New York: Crown Trade Paperbacks, 1994.

Ting-Toomey, Stela, ed. *The Challenge of Facework: Cross-Cultural and Interpersonal Issues*. Albany: State University of New York Press, 1994.

Wainwright, Gordon R. *Body Language (Teach Yourself)*. Lincolnwood, IL: NTC Publishing Group, 1993.

Wolfgang, Aaron. *Everybody's Guide to People Watching*. Yarmouth, ME: Intercultural Press, 1995.

IDEAS FOR DEVELOPMENT:

- a video of body language and gestures of different countries
- a study of the silent messages conveyed by body language and gestures
- a storyboard with comparisons of various common gestures and their meanings in different countries
- role-playing to demonstrate ways of greeting, beckoning waiters, etc. in different countries

DID YOU KNOW?

Our gesture of a circle formed with thumb and forefinger to signify "OK" is extremely offensive in Italy, Greece, Spain, and Ukraine. In France it signals "zero" or "worthless." Our "V" for victory sign, if made with the palm facing inward, is very offensive in England.

Title: Habitat for Humanity

Content Areas: Social Studies
Tech. Ed.
Family and Consumer Science

BACKGROUND:

Habitat for Humanity seeks to eliminate poverty housing and hopelessness and to make decent housing a matter of conscience and action. Started in 1976, HFH draws people from all walks of life together to build houses with families in need. Volunteer labor and tax-deductible donations of cash and materials have resulted in more than 75,000 houses being built or rehabilitated around the world and more than 375,000 people having decent, affordable housing in more than 2,000 communities. Active in every state, HFH provides no-interest mortgages to each homeowner who is required to invest 400 "sweat equity" hours into the construction of their own house or other HFH homes.

REFERENCES:

Fuller, Millard. *A Simple, Decent Place to Live*. Dallas: Word Pub., 1995.

Fuller, Millard, and Diane Scott. *No More Shacks*. Waco, TX: Word Books, 1986.

Fuller, Millard, and Linda Fuller. *The Excitement Is Building*. Dallas: Word Publications, 1990.

Gaillard, Frye. *If I Were a Carpenter*. Winston-Salem, NC: John F. Blair, Publisher, 1996.

Purks, James. *Habitat for Humanity*. Atlanta, GA: Habitat for Humanity, 1991.

IDEAS FOR DEVELOPMENT:

- a computer presentation of costs of all labor and materials to build an "average" house
- a comparison of costs of HFH "Green Team" houses and "normal" house construction
- an analysis of substandard housing in your town and the agencies charged with oversight
- a photo display of tasks in home-building that can be done by volunteers and itemize the savings
- a storyboard of HFH projects in your area

DID YOU KNOW?

Nearly 30 million U.S. households face one or more of these housing problems: cost burdens (paying over 30% of monthly income for rent and utilities); overcrowding (more people than rooms in dwelling); physical inadequacy (no hot water, no electricity, no toilet).

Title: Armor through the Ages

Content Areas: History
Tech. Ed.

BACKGROUND:

Armor is nearly as old as warfare itself. Garments made from leather or quilted cloth were the only protection for the earliest soldiers, but brigandine armor (small linked metal plates covered with cloth and studded with metal rivets) was used before the introduction of metal breastplates in the 1st century AD. Japanese, Chinese, and Greek warriors were protected by armor well before that time. Chain mail was worn by the Normans in 1000 AD. Whole body armor was in use in Europe by 1420. These suits of armor could weigh over 50 pounds and getting them on could take an hour. Armor has evolved as armaments and weapons have changed—to include protection from lasers and chemical and biological agents.

REFERENCES:

Bottomly, Ian. *Arms and Armor of the Samurai.* New York: Crescent Books, 1996.

Edge, David. *Arms and Armor of the Medieval Knight.* Avenel, NJ: Crescent Books, 1995.

Gilbert, Adrian. *Arms and Armor.* Brookfield, CT: Millbrook Press, 1997.

Shadrake, Dan, and Susanna Shadrake. *Barbarian Warriors: Saxons, Vikings, Normans.* London: Brasseys, Inc., 1997.

Snodgrass, Anthony. *Arms and Armor of the Greeks.* Baltimore: Johns Hopkins University Press, 1998.

IDEAS FOR DEVELOPMENT:

- a storyboard of the evolution of armor from ancient through modern Kevlar
- a display of drawings depicting armor and its components from different time periods
- a computer presentation of the evolution of the gorget or the helmet
- an analysis of how changes in warfare methods affected armor construction
- a study of historical efforts to protect the face, eyes, head, and respiration

---

DID YOU KNOW?

Although many volunteers wore "bullet-proof" steel chest-plates during the Civil War, the Army did not officially issue body armor until WW II when aircrews received armored vests. Foot soldiers were not issued body armor in the form of flak jackets until 1952 in Korea.

Title: The "Great American Desert"

Content Areas: Science
History

BACKGROUND:

Prior to the 1860s the American Great Plains, a semiarid shortgrass habitat, was know as the Great American Desert. The designation of "desert" was not strictly accurate, but it was correct in that patterns of rainfall could be very erractic and almost desertlike at times. The name "Great Plains" came into general use after the 1860s as a result of propaganda by the railway companies who wished to see the plains settled and thereby create business for the trains. The subsequent influx of pioneer farmers turned the grassland into an agricultural and cattle and sheep grazing region. The Great Drought (immortalized by John Steinbeck in *The Grapes of Wrath* began in 1933 and lasted until 1942. The predrought abundance and distribution of native fauna and flora returned only after 1960.

REFERENCES:

Houle, Mary. *The Prairie Keepers: Secrets of the Grassland*. Reading, MA: Addison-Wesley, 1995.

Joem, Anthony, ed. *The Changing Prairie: North American Grasslands*. London: Oxford University Press, 1995.

Manning, Richard. *Grassland: The History, Biology, Politics, and Promise of the American Prairie*. New York: Penguin, USA, 1997.

Smith, Robert Leo. *Ecology and Field Biology*. New York: HarperCollins College Publishers, 1996.

Steele, Philip. *Grasslands*. Minneapolis: Carolrhoda Books, 1997.

IDEAS FOR DEVELOPMENT:

- a storyboard depicting advertisements and propaganda used to entice settlers
- a video of before-and-after pictures of the development of the grasslands
- an analysis of the adaptations of grassland plants and animals
- a study of the effects of the Great Drought of the 1930s on farm families

> ### DID YOU KNOW?
>
> 50 million bison which survived year-round solely on prairie grasses populated the American grassland until the late 1800s. Gradually prairies became home to ranches with 45 million climatically unsuited cattle and sheep that now consume 70% of the U.S. grain production.

Ideas for More Independent Projects

Content Area: Art

1. Create pop-up books on various subjects (reference: artist, Robert Sabuda)
2. Paint a subject in the style of the Old Masters and explain each style.
3. Paint one subject and interpret it in each of the classical styles; Impressionism, Abstract Expressionism, etc.
4. Art in nature, chemistry, biology, or physics.
6. Analyze art during WW II.
7. Detailed sketches or paintings of Christmas tree decorations through U.S. history or of different countries.
8. Research the history and the subsequent evolution of the phenakistiscope.
9. Famous fakers of paintings (e.g., the Vermeer fakes during WW II).
10. The history and biography of famous artists.

Content Area: Business

1. The history of a successful small business in your city.
2. Research and develop a theoretical investment portfolio for a personal college fund and follow its progress for a period of time.
3. How to start a new business.
4. What impact the Pennsylvania turnpike had on life in small towns along its path.
5. What is involved in running a restaurant (licenses, advertising, supplies, accounts, etc.)
6. Design travel tours with actual time frames, logistics, costs.
7. Take an invention through the patent process (hypothetically or actually).
8. How is a newscast put together?
9. The history of famous logos or symbols (Uncle Sam, the Nike swoosh, etc.).

Content Area: Engineering

1. The architectural design of Arabic buildings that provide for natural air conditioning.
2. The engineering in WW II (Operation Mulberry, Bailey bridges, etc.).
3. An analysis of local architecture over the past centuries.
4. The engineering of bridges.
5. Tunnel engineering.
6. Engineering changes in bicycles.
7. Ergonomics.

8. The evolution of radar.
9. Engineering changes in cars.
10. Virtual reality.
11. The encryption of messages in wartime (ancient use of signals, the M209 coding machine, and Enigma).
12. The impact of the Chinese dam on the Yangtze River.
13. Fuzzy logic.

Content Area: English

1. Analysis of a Civil War diary.
2. A study of when proverbs were popular, what they taught, and when they were taught in schools.
3. Analysis of new fad words and slang (e.g., "parse" and "egregious" became popular in 1998).
4. The etymology of animal names (e.g., giraffe is Arabic for "tallest of all"; cheetah is Hindu for "spotted one").
5. The origin of words such as mettle, meddle, metal, medal, and false cognates.

Content Area: Family and Consumer Science

1. Learn and teach the "old Games" such as jacks, tops, hoops, marbles.
2. Hair styles during the last century.
3. How the customs and traditions of mourning the dead have changed over time.
4. A study of the changes in etiquette.
5. The history of military uniform design (e.g., the Zouaves during the Civil War, the "pinks" of WW II, the Vatican Swiss Guard).
6. A history of fragrances and how they reflect various aspects of society.
7. How food rationing during WW II impacted cooking style and recipes.
8. Dating customs across generations and cultures.
9. Write the biography of a Senior Citizen (life experiences, attitudes, career choices, work, leisure, discipline, school, entertainment).
10. The history of Spam®; people in England still love it because it was the only meat they had with any regularity during WW II and Nikita Khrushchev said "Spam saved the Soviet Union during WW II."
11. What studies have concluded about the relationship of socioeconomic status and health.

Content Area: Foreign Language

1. A talk show with exchange students.

2. Contrast body language and gestures of Hispanics and Europeans.
3. Festivals, celebrations, holidays in another culture.
4. Family life and relationships of several cultures.
5. Interview Hispanic families who move from big eastern cities to rural areas (problems they encounter and their reasons for relocating).
6. Create a translation booklet for recent immigrants.
7. The heritage of the Mennonites.

Content Area: History

1. What were the effects of the war in Bosnia or Vietnam on schools and students?
2. The history of the people who first settled in your town.
3. The life of children of coal miners in the last century.
4. The difficulties experienced by children of illegal aliens.
5. The contribution of women in the various wars (the Revolutionary War, the Crimean War, the Civil War, WW I).
6. How would history have been different if the British had won the Revolutionary War?
7. How would history have been different if Napoleon had won the Battle of Waterloo?
8. How would U.S. history have been different if the South had won the Civil War?
9. How would history have been different if Lincoln had not been assassinated?
10. How would history have been different if the Axis Powers had won WW II?
11. How would history have been different if the Allies had not had the Japanese secret code?
12. U.S. territories/possessions; do they want to be states?
13. The history of your town.
14. A study of local Native American culture in your area.
15. Interviews with WW II veterans or Vietnam War veterans.

Content Area: Mathematics

1. A study of mathematics in war (range finding, radar, optics, navigation, shipping, tonnage, logistics, ballistics).
2. Geometry in Arabic art or Native American art.
3. The statistics of crime (full moon, speed limits, etc.).
4. Chaos theory.
5. Contributions from other cultures to mathematics (e.g., the concept of zero from Arabic scholars).
6. How various professions utilize mathematics.
7. Analyze the impact of inexpensive calculators on elementary and secondary education.

8. The historical use of mathematics in navigation of aircraft and ships; and how computers are used for this purpose today.
9. Fibonacci sequences in nature.
10. Symmetry in nature (bilateral, radial, pentagonal, tri-fold rotational, 4-fold rotational, etc.).
11. The mathematics of chemistry or physics.
12. Hexagonal packing.
13. The mathematics of spirals in nature.

Content Area: Multidisciplinary

1. Write the biography of teenage parents.
2. The life story of recent immigrants.
3. The archaeology of trash.
4. The history of local fishing or hunting.
5. The validity of old wives' tales.
6. New products that emerged from WW II.
7. New products that emerged from the space program.
8. Solutions to the National Park crisis.
9. A study of propaganda in poster art and advertising during WW II.
10. A brochure of your state's "firsts" or "mosts" (the first to elect a woman senator, the most covered bridges, etc.).
11. What is it really like to be a _____ (interview people with various careers to discover their training, frustrations, etc.).
12. A study of unusual hobbies.
13. Reconstruct a journey along the old route 66, 40, or 30 and show the changes in towns, motels, restaurants, etc.
14. Changes in long distance telephone service and its use.
15. Time capsules: study others and make one (actually or virtually on a computer).

Content Area: Music

1. The history of jazz, bluegrass, etc.
2. The music of DNA.
3. How the music in WW II reflected the ideas of the time.
4. What scientific research has been done to show a link between early exposure to music and mathematical ability.
5. Why clogging is like the Irish jig and why it has Spanish and Arabic overtones.
6. Music therapy.
7. The mathematics of classical music.

Content Area: Science

1. Science fair projects (see appendix B for source books).
2. An analysis of blood splatters as a crime scene investigatory method.
3. Do cicada chirps actually predict hot weather or are they merely a result of the time of year and time of mating?
4. A study of changes in the population of game animals in your state.
5. Medical treatment during the Crimean War or Revolutionary War.
6. What animal signals occur before earthquakes?
7. How effective are old home remedies?
8. An investigation of local problems with weeds and crops (eg. soybeans and black nightshade).
9. The ecology of native plants or imported plants.
10. Is there a relationship between IQ and having an imaginary friend as a child?
11. Study local agricultural practices of the past.
12. Medicines and cures from other cultures.
13. The ethical questions of the genetic engineering revolution.
14. Bird watching.
15. The history and uses of pendulums.
16. A brochure and map to locate and identify mushrooms, wildflowers, trees, etc. in your area.
17. How comets are discovered.
18. Research the rivalry between early alternating current (AC) proponents and direct current (DC) supporters.
19. New forensic tools: entomology, tests for poisons (cyanide).
20. Help a class of elementary students with their science fair projects.
21. The evolution of clocks.
22. How the pollution of modern life has changed the weather on weekends.

Content Area: Social Studies

1. A day in the life of ___ (social worker, veterinarian, lawyer, etc.).
2. Follow a land development plan from beginning to end with your local Planning Commission.
3. How does your local Zoning Commission function.
4. Write an account of the activities of one week in your local township government.
5. The history of migrant workers in your area.
6. The history of the creation of a state or territory such as Nunavut.
7. Interview the teenagers of yesteryears.
8. What laws, traditions, and expenses are involved in local elections?

Content Area: Tech. Ed.

1. The history of parachute rigging.
2. Landscape design for your neighborhood.
3. Evolution of ammunition, Minié balls, black powder arms, etc.
4. The technology of a landfill.
5. Determination of the most economical, environmentally safe, effective lawn or golf course fertilizer for your area.
6. How is a land survey conducted.
7. Study Mission furniture style (or another style) and build a piece of furniture in that style.
8. Compare the cost of restoring an old building or house in your area to the cost of tearing it down.
9. How is the individuality of telegraph or wireless operators known?
10. The evolution of military communications technology.
11. How are cipher specialists in the military trained?
12. How a billboard is made; from design to construction.
13. The history of the Ford Mustang.
14. The evolution of the fax machine.
15. How cold weather survival clothing and equipment are designed.

Appendix A

Independent Project Approval Form

The student must have this Approval Form completed and signed before beginning the Independent Project.

Student's Name _____

Independent Project Title _____

Attach the Independent Project Proposal to this form.

This project involves :   ☐ **Human Subjects**
                                 ☐ **Nonhuman Vertebrate Animals**
                                 ☐ **Pathogenic Agents** (including bacteria, viruses, fungi)
                                 ☐ **Hazardous Chemicals** (including flammable, explosive, toxic, carcinogenic, or mutagenic chemicals
                                 ☐ **Hazardous Equipment** (including lasers, welders, high-voltage equipment, firearms and other weapons or munitions, and radioactive substances)

This project does not involve any of the research area listed above ☐

Advisor's Printed Name _____

Advisor's Signature _____ Date _____

If a mentor is assisting the student:
Mentor's Printed Name _____

Mentor's Signature _____ Date _____

Parent/Guardian Printed Name _____

Parent/Guardian Signature _____ Date _____

Principal's Printed Name _____

Principal's Signature _____ Date _____

School Nurse's Printed Name _____

School Nurse's Signature _____ Date _____

Informed Consent Form

The student must have this Informed Consent Form signed before beginning work with human subjects (including surveys and questionnaires).

Student's Name _____

Independent Project Title _____

Attach the Independent Project Proposal to this form.

Advisor's or Mentor's Printed Name _____

Advisor's or Mentor's Signature _____ Date _____

Principal's Printed Name _____

Principal's Signature _____ Date _____

School Nurse's Printed Name _____

School Nurse's Signature _____ Date _____

To be completed by each human subject prior to participation:

☐ I consent to participate in the project and I understand that I am free to withdraw my consent and to withdraw from participation at any time.

☐ I consent to the use of visual images (e.g., photographs, videorecordings) involving my participation in this project (optional).

Participant's Printed Name _____

Participant's Signature _____ Date _____

If the participant is under 18 years of age, a parent/guardian signature is required.

Parent/Guardian Printed Name _____

Parent/Guardian Signature _____ Date _____

Progress Checklist for Advisor/Mentor

The advisor/mentor may use this checklist to monitor the progress of preparation.

Student Name _____

Independent Project Title _____

ITEM	complete	not yet complete
1. Reviewed criteria with student		
2. Focus of study is stated		
3. Purpose and objectives stated		
4. Described plan for gathering information		
5. Described a procedure for completing the project		
6. Provided a time line for completing the project		
7. Resources and materials listed		
8. Description of product or presentation given		
9. Evaluation criteria listed		
10. Required signatures have been obtained		

Comments:

Independent Project Evaluation Form

Student Name _____

Independent Project Title _____

	Best .... Worst				
	5	4	3	2	1
Presentation (overall)					
logically organized and clearly communicated					
sufficient depth of ideas					
support materials/audio visuals					
Presenter (overall)					
audible					
prepared					
motivated					
knowledgeable					
confident					
Product (overall)					
quality					
a natural extension of the research					
interesting					
Documentation (overall)					
evidence that research has been conducted					
appropriate strategies used					
displays clarity and organization					
Research Paper (overall)					
displays clarity and organization					
quality					
sufficient depth of ideas					
correct grammar and spelling					
references cited and adequate					
interesting					
logically organized					

Appendix B

Sources

Asimov, Isaac. *Astronomy Projects*. Milwaukee, WI: Gareth Stevens Pub., 1996.

Banfield, Susan. *What in the World*. Mahwah, NJ: Troll Associates, 1992.

Bonnett, Robert L., and Daniel Keen. *Computers: 49 Science Fair Projects*. Blue Ridge Summit, PA: TAB Books, 1990.

———. *Earth Science: 49 Science Fair Projects*. Blue Ridge Summit, PA: TAB Books, 1990.

———. *Environmental Science: 49 ScienceFair Projects*. Blue Ridge Summit, PA: TAB Books, 1990.

Cohen, Marcus S., Edward D. Gaughan, Arthur Knoebel, Douglas Kurtz, and David J. Pengelley. *Student Research Projects in Calculus*. Washington, DC: Mathematical Assn. of America, 1991.

Coveney, Peter, and Roger Highfield. *Frontiers in Complexity*. New York: Fawcett Books, 1996.

Cox, Shirley. *Chemistry*. Vero Beach, FL: Rourke Publishers, 1993.

Crane, Julia G., and Michael V. Angrosino. *Field Projects in Anthropology: A Student Handbook*. Prospect Heights, IL: Waveland Press, 1992.

Dashefsky, H. Steve. *Botany: High-School ScienceFair Projects*. Blue Ridge Summit, PA: TAB Books, 1995.

———. *Entomology: High-School Science Fair Projects*. Blue Ridge Summit, PA: TAB Books, 1994.

———. *Microbiology: High-School Science Fair Projects*. Blue Ridge Summit, PA: TAB Books, 1995.

———. *Zoology: High-School Science Fair Projects*. Blue Ridge Summit, PA: TAB Books, 1995.

Duncan, Nancy. *Entrepreneurship*. Englewood Cliffs, NJ: Silver Burdett Press, 1990.

Gardner, Robert, and Eric Kemer. *Making and Using Scientific Models*. New York: Franklin Watts, 1993.

Millspaugh, Ben. *Aviation and Space Projects*. Blue Ridge Summit, PA: TAB Books, 1992.

Mogil, H. Michael. *The Amateur Meteorologist*. New York: Watts, 1993.

Newton, David E. *Making and Using Scientific Equipment*. New York: Watts, 1991.

O'Neil, Karen. *Health and Medicine Projects for Young Scientists*. New York: Franklin Watts, 1997.

Orwig, Ann H. "Bridging the Ages with Help from Technology." *Technology & Learning* 16, no. 1 (September 1995): 26-33.

Reid, William. *Studio Projects in Art History*. Portland, ME: J. Weston Walch, 1990.

Roets Lois. *Student Projects: Ideas and Plans*. Des Moines, IA: Leadership Publishers, 1994.

———. *Survey and Public Opinion Research: A Student Manual*. Des Moines, IA: Leadership Publishers, 1987.

Sanzo, Janet. *Make Your Own Video*. Lincolnwood, IL: Publication International, 1991.

Sima, Patricia. *Immigration*. Huntington Beach, CA: Teacher Created Materials, Inc., 1993.

Wee, Patricia Hachten. *Science Fair Projects for Elementary Schools*. Lanham, MD: Scarecrow Press, 1999.

————. *Managing Successful Science Fair Projects*. Portland, ME: J. Weston Walch, 1996.

Wheeler, Ben. *Countries and Cultures*. Huntington Beach, CA: Teacher Created Materials, Inc., 1994.

Wiggers, Ray. *The Amateur Geologist*. New York: Watts, 1993.

Williamson, Susan. "Roots in the Classroom." *Book Report* 9, no. 3 (November-December 1990): 31-34.

Index

D

E

F

About the Author

Patricia Hachten Wee (M.S.Ed., Temple University) has taught scientific research, ecology, environmental science, biology, and physical science. She has advised high school students with independent projects/graduation projects for many years. Science fair project work has been a major component of her school's curriculum, and she has advised and encouraged students in this work for most of her teaching career. She is the author of *Managing Successful Science Fair Projects* (J. Weston Walch, 1996) and *Science Fair Projects for Elementary Schools* (Scarecrow Press, 1998). Her high school students are regularly finalists in the International Science and Engineering Fair, the Intel Science Talent Search, the Dupont Science Essay Competition, the Junior Science and Humanities Symposium, and other national competitions.

Mrs. Wee and her husband reside in Lancaster County, Pennsylvania, and have five grown children and three grandchildren.

373.139　Wee, Patricia
Wee　　　Hachten, 1948-

Independent projects,
step by step.

DATE			